Quick

Greek

Teach Yourself edition first published 1987
Third impression 1988
Copyright © 1987
Hodder and Stoughton Ltd
Adapted from the original Langenscheidt edition by E. Savani.
Langenscheidt edition by Diethard Lübke, copyright © 1984 by
Langenscheidt KG, Berlin and Munich
Illustrations by Herbert Horn.

British Library Cataloguing in Publication Data

Lübke, Diethard
    Quick & easy Greek.—(Teach yourself books)
    1. Greek language, Modern—Spoken Greek
    I. Title
    489′.383421   PA1059
    ISBN 0 340 38766 1

Typeset by Santype International Ltd., Salisbury
Printed in Great Britain for
Hodder and Stoughton Educational,
a division of Hodder and Stoughton Ltd,
Mill Road, Dunton Green, Sevenoaks, Kent,
by Richard Clay Ltd, Bungay, Suffolk

Quick & Easy
Greek

Diethard Lübke

TEACH YOURSELF BOOKS
Hodder and Stoughton

Contents

Contents

Introduction

This course of self-study aims to help you understand and speak simple Modern Greek, the sort of Greek you will need on a visit to Greece. It cannot promise that at the end you will be speaking perfectly, but by enabling you to learn the most important words and expressions a visitor needs, it will undoubtedly help to improve your experience of Greece and enable you to get more out of your time abroad.

The course does not require a great deal of study or concentration, but it does offer more than a phrasebook and you will find that if you are prepared to spend a certain amount of time, even at odd hours of the day, in going through each unit, learning the alphabet and testing your knowledge carefully, you will begin to acquire a basic knowledge of the language. Then take the book with you on your trip abroad, so that you can practise the words and phrases you have learnt. Don't be afraid to use them—you are bound to make mistakes, but the most important thing is that you will have made yourself understood.

The course consists of 20 units, each dealing with a particular aspect of a visit to Greece. Each unit is based on carefully selected Greek words and phrases, next to each of which is its phonetic equivalent, aimed at helping you to pronounce the words accurately, and its English translation. These phonetic transliterations may either be used as an alternative to learning the Greek alphabet or as an aid to mastering it, depending on how seriously you want to learn the language. Look at each phrase carefully and read it aloud, referring to the Greek alphabet where necessary. The exercises which follow are of two types: those which require a test of memory, to see if you have remembered a word or phrase which occurred on a previous page, and those which ask you to adapt a given phrase or sentence to suit your own purposes. If you find, gradually, that you are beginning to be able to do this, you are passing the 'acid test' of learning a language, which is being able to adapt given language patterns to any situation you choose.

At the end of each unit is a short information section in English which you will find useful on your visit.

The course expects very little knowledge of grammar, but readers who are interested in learning how the language works will find the introduction to Greek grammar useful. This contains some of the basic elements of grammar, mainly those illustrated in the course. A careful study of the Pronunciation section is advised, because although there can be no substitute for listening to Greeks speaking their own language, it is possible to give a fairly good approximation of individual sounds. It is a good idea to read both these sections before starting the course, and then to refer to them frequently.

How to Speak Greek

1   In Modern Greek words of more than one syllable carry an accent mark (΄). The mark shows that the accented syllable is stressed more than the others. The mark can be on any of the syllables:

κύριος   kírios   *Mr*
κυρία   kiría   *Mrs*
καλά   kalá   *well*

You may sometimes see words written according to the old (pre-1982) system, whereby there were three different accent marks (΄) (`) (˜). All of them indicated the same thing: the syllable to be stressed within the word. (During 1974–1982 the spelling system was reformed and the accentuation simplified to include only the one accent.)

2   There are no long or short vowels in Modern Greek. All vowels are of equal duration.

3   Unlike Ancient Greek where a combination of two vowels (diphthong) was pronounced as two distinct sounds, in Modern Greek the same vowel combination is pronounced as one sound:

Ancient Greek: πολλοί polói   *many*
Modern Greek: πολλοί polí   *many*

4   Pay special attention to the consonants which look like English ones but are pronounced differently:

β in Greek is pronounced like English *v*:

βάζο   vázo   *vase*

ν in Greek is pronounced like English *n*:

ναι   ne   *yes*

ρ in Greek is pronounced like English *r*:

ρεκόρ   rekór   *record*

5 The Greek question mark (;) is written like the English semicolon:

Τι κάνετε; ti kánete   *How are you?*

6 Some signs written in capital letters (often names of shops) end in N, which, however, is not pronounced in spoken Greek:

ΚΑΦΕΝΕΙΟΝ (*café*) written kafeníon, pronounced kafenío.

ΕΣΤΙΑΤΟΡΙΟΝ (*restaurant*) written estiatórion, pronounced estiatório.

The Greek Alphabet

Letter				*Transliteration symbol*
Α	α		(álfa)	a
Β	β		(víta)	v
Γ	γ		(ghála)	gh
			(Before ι or ε sound)	y
Δ	δ		(**thé**lta)	**th**
Ε	ε		(épsilon)	e
Ζ	ζ		(zíta)	z
Η	η		(íta)	i
Θ	ϑ		(thíta)	th
Ι	ι		(yóta)	i
Κ	κ		(kápa)	k
Λ	λ		(lám**th**a)	l
Μ	μ		(mi)	m
Ν	ν		(ni)	n
Ξ	ξ		(ksi)	ks
Ο	ο		(ómikron)	o
Π	π		(pi)	p
Ρ	ρ		(ro)	r
Σ	σ	ς	(sígma)	s
Τ	τ		(taf)	t
Υ	υ		(ípsilon)	i
Φ	φ		(fi)	f
Χ	χ		(hi)	h
Ψ	ψ		(psi)	ps
Ω	ω		(omégha)	o

Note that the letter ς is used only at the end of a word:

κύριος kírios *Mr*   δεσποινίς **th**espinís *Miss*

Greek pronunciation
Vowel sounds

Practise saying these words

α	like *a* in *car*	άσπρο áspro	*white*
		κρασί krasí	*wine*
ε	like *e* in *pen*	εδώ ethó	*here*
		νερό neró	*water*
η, ι, υ	like *i* in *machine*	σήμερα símera	*today*
		τυρί tirí	*cheese*
ο, ω	like *o* in *top*	τώρα tóra	*now*
		ομελέττα omeléta	*omelette*

Vowel combinations

αι	like *e* in *pen*	ναι ne	*yes*
		και ke	*and*
ει	like *i* in *machine*	είκοσι íkosi	*twenty*
		εκεί ekí	*there*
οι	like *i* in *machine*	δεσποινίς thespinís	*Miss*
		πολλοί polí	*many*
ου	like *oo* in *food*	μπλούζα bloóza	*blouse*
		σαμπουάν sampooán	*shampoo*
αυ, ευ	like *af, ef* (before ϑ, κ, ξ, π, σ, τ, φ, χ)	αυτοκίνητο aftokínito	*car*
αυ, ευ	like *av, ev* (before β, γ, δ, ζ, λ, μ, ν, ρ)	αυγό avghó	*egg*

Consonants

β	like *v* in *very*	βαλίτσα valítsa	*suitcase*
		βουνό voonó	*mountain*
γ	like *g* in *give*	γαρίδα gharítha	*prawn*
		αγόρι aghóri	*boy*
	like *y* in *yes* (before ι or e sound)	γεύμα yévma	*meal*
		γιατρός yatrós	*doctor*
δ	like *th* in *this*	δέκα théka	*ten*
		εδώ ethó	*here*
ζ	like *z* in *zoo*	ζάχαρη záhari	*sugar*
		ζώνη zóni	*belt*
ϑ	like *th* in *thin*	θάλασσα thálasa	*sea*
		θέλω thélo	*I want*
κ	like *k* in *key*	εκατό ekató	*one hundred*
		κιλό kiló	*kilo*

λ	like *l* in *love*	πορτοκάλι	portokáli	*orange*
		λεπτό	leptó	*minute*
μ	like *m* in *man*	μενού	menoó	*menu*
		κρέμα	kréma	*cream*
ν	like *n* in *new*	πεπόνι	pepóni	*melon*
		νύχτα	níhta	*night*
ξ	like *ks* in *six*	ξεναγός	ksenaghós	*(tourist) guid*e
		ξενοδοχείο	ksenothohío	*hotel*
π	like *p* in *post*	παγωτό	paghotó	*ice-cream*
		αποσκευές	aposkevés	*luggage*
ρ	like *r* in *red*	μπύρα	bíra	*beer*
		παραλία	paralía	*beach*
σ, ς	like *s* in *sun*	είκοσι	íkosi	*twenty*
		σαπούνι	sapoóni	*soap*
τ	like *t* in *top*	τώρα	tóra	*now*
		βούτυρο	voótiro	*butter*
φ	like *f* in *fun*	φούστα	foósta	*skirt*
		εφτά	eftá	*seven*
χ	like *h* in *hat*	χάρτης	hártis	*map*
		χρόνος	hrónos	*year*
ψ	like *ps* in *lapse*	ψάρι	psári	*fish*
		ψωμί	psomí	*bread*

Combinations of consonants

μπ	like *b* in *beer*	μπισκότα	biskóta	*biscuits*
		μπλε	ble	*blue*
	like *mb* in *ember*	ομπρέλλα	ombrélla	*umbrella*
ντ	like *d* in *dear*	ντομάτα	domáta	*tomato*
		ντους	doos	*shower*
	like *nd* in *land*	κοντά	kondá	*near*
		δέντρο	théndro	*tree*
γκ	like *g* in *go*	γκαρσόν	garsón	*waiter*
		γκρι	gri	*gray*
γγ	like *ng* in *angle*	αγγελία	angelía	*announcement*
		αγγούρι	angoóri	*cucumber*
τσ	like *ts* in *lots*	ρετσίνα	retsína	*resinated wine*
		τσιγάρα	tsighára	*cigarettes*
τζ	like *j* in *john*	μελιτζάνα	melijána	*aubergine*
		τζατζίκι	jajíki	*yoghurt salad*

Note that all Greek letters are sounded and all vowels are pronounced distinctly (even when they are unstressed or at the end of a word).

Introduction to Greek Grammar

In Modern Greek all articles, nouns and adjectives belong to one of three basic groups: masculine, feminine or neuter. A masculine noun is accompanied by a form of the masculine article (**o** = *the*, **ἐναζ** = *a/an*), a feminine noun is accompanied by a feminine article (**η** = *the*, **μία** = *a/an*) and a neuter noun is accompanied by a neuter article (**το** = *the*, **ἐνα** = *a/an*).

o άντρας	*the man*	**ἐναζ** πατέρας	*a father*
η γυναίκα	*the woman*	**μία** πόρτα	*a door*
το παιδί	*the child*	**ἐνα** δωμάτιο	*a room*

In addition to these three basic groups, the particular form which a Greek word takes in any particular sentence is dictated by its position and function within that sentence. There are three functions: nominative (subject), genitive (possessive = of the) and accusative (object).

Note also that a singular noun takes the singular form of the article or adjective, and a plural noun takes a plural article or adjective.

1 Articles
Definite article 'the'

Singular		*Masculine*	*Feminine*	*Neuter*
nom.	*the*	o o	η i	το to
gen.	*of the*	του too	της tis	του too
acc.	*the*	το(ν) ton	τη(ν) tin	το to

Plural				
nom.	*the*	οι i	οι i	τα ta
gen.	*of the*	των ton	των ton	των ton
acc.	*the*	τους toos	τις tis	τα ta

Indefinite article 'a/an'

		Masculine	*Feminine*	*Neuter*
nom.	*a/an*	ἐνας énas	μία mía	ἐνα éna
gen.	*of a/an*	ενός enós	μιάς myás	ενός enós
acc.	*a/an*	ἐνα éna	μία mía	ἐνα éna

The indefinite article **ένας, μία, ένα** can be omitted in everyday spoken Greek:

θέλω καφέ (instead of θέλω ένα καφέ). *I would like a coffee.*

2 Nouns

As we have seen, all Greek nouns belong to one of three basic groups. They may be classified according to the following groups of endings:

Singular	Masculine	Feminine	Neuter
nom.	−ος, −ας, −ης	−α, −η	−ο, −ι, −μα
gen.	−ου, −α, −η	−ας, −ης	−ου, −ιού, −ματος
acc.	−ο, −α, −η	−α, −η	−ο, −ι, −μα
Plural			
nom.	−οι, −ες, −ες	−ες, −ες	−α, −ια, −ματα
gen.	−ων, −ων, −ων	−ων, −ων	−ων, −ιών, −ματων
acc.	−ους, −ες, −ες	−ες, −ες	−α, −ια, −ματα

Here are some examples of nouns and articles:

Singular

n.   **ο** άντρα**ς**   *the man*   **η** γυναίκα   *the woman*

g.   το όνομα **του** άντρα   το όνομα **της** γυναίκα**ς**
the name of the man   *the name of the woman*

a.   ξέρω **τον** άντρα   ξέρω **την** γυναίκα
I know the man   *I know the woman*

> *n.*   **το** παιδί   *the child*
>
> *g.*   το όνομα **του** παιδ**ιού**
> *the name of the child*
>
> *a.*   ξέρω **το** παιδί
> *I know the child*

Plural

n.   **οι** άντρε**ς** *the men*   **οι** γυναίκε**ς** *the women*

g.   τα ονόματα **των** αντρών   τα ονόματα **των** γυναικών
the names of the men   *the names of the women*

a.   ξέρω **τους** άντρες   ξέρω **τις** γυναίκες
I know the men   *I know the women*

> *n.*   **τα** παιδ**ιά** *the children*
>
> *g.*   τα ονόματα **των** παιδιών
> *the names of the children*
>
> *a.*   ξέρω **τα** παιδιά
> *I know the children*

The definite article is used with the names and titles of people, but it is omitted when addressing someone directly. Here are some examples of its use with names and titles:

Ο **Νίκος** είναι γιατρός.   *Nikos is a doctor.*
Ο **κύριος** Σμιθ είναι δικηγόρος.   *Mr Smith is a lawyer.*
Η **κυρία** Σμιθ είναι δασκάλα.   *Mrs Smith is a teacher.*

Το αυτοκίνητο **του Νίκου** είναι άσπρο.   *Nikos's car is white.*
Το πορτοφόλι **του κυρίου** Σμιθ είναι εδώ.   *Mr Smith's wallet is here.*
Η βαλίτσα **της κυρίας** Σμιθ είναι εδώ.   *Mrs Smith's suitcase is here.*

and here are some examples of its omission:

Καλημέρα, Νίκο.   *Good morning, Niko.*
Καλησπέρα, κυρία Σμίθ.   *Good afternoon, Mrs Smith.*

It is also usual for names of places, countries, towns, islands, etc. to be preceded by the definite article.

η Ελλάδα   *Greece*
η Αθήνα   *Athens*
η Κρήτη   *Crete*

3   Adjectives

In Greek the endings of adjectives change according to whether the nouns they accompany are masculine, feminine, neuter, singular or plural. The form they take is also dependent on their function within the sentence, which may, in any particular case, be either nominative, genitive or accusative.

The basic adjective endings are: *masc.* –**ος**, *fem.* –**η** or –**α**, *neut.* –**ο**:

ο καλ**ός** καιρός   *the good weather*
η ωραί**α** θάλασσα   *the beautiful sea*
το ακριβ**ό** κρασί   *the expensive wine*

4   Prepositions

Prepositions in Modern Greek are followed by the accusative form of the noun. One of the most commonly used prepositions is **σε**, which has several meanings (*on, in, at, to, into*).

When preceding a definite article, the two words contract to produce the following forms:

masc. **στο(ν)**
fem. **στη(ν)** } *on the, in the, at the, to the, into the*
neut. **στο**

Unless the word following **στον** and **στην** begins with a vowel, the final letter **ν** is often left out:

Πάω **στο(ν)** σταθμό. *I go to the station.*
Μένω **στην** Αθήνα. *I live in Athens.*

5 I, you, etc.
The personal pronouns **I**, **you**, **he**, etc., although they have equivalent forms in Greek, are not commonly used (except for emphasis):

εγώ	eghó	*I*	εμείς	emís	*we*
εσύ	esí	*you* (familiar)	εσείς	esís	*you* (formal)
αυτός	aftós	*he*	αυτοί	aftí	*they* (masc.)
αυτή	aftí	*she*	αυτές	aftés	*they* (fem.)
αυτό	aftó	*it*	αυτά	aftá	*they* (neut.)

6 This and That
Demonstratives *this* [**αυτός** aftós (masc.), **αυτή** aftí (fem.), **αυτό** aftó (neut.))] and *that* (**εκείνος** ekínos (masc.), **εκείνη** ekíni (fem.), **εκείνο** ekíno (neut.)]] behave like other adjectives in Greek and change their form according to the same rules. They are usually placed *before* the noun, which is preceded by its definite article:

αυτός ο άντρας *this man*
αυτή η βαλίτσα *this suitcase*
αυτό το κρασί *this wine*

7 My, your, etc.
The possessive adjectives **my**, **your**, **his**, etc., are placed *after* the noun, which should be preceded by its definite article:

ο αναπτήρας **μου** *my lighter*
η τσάντα **σου** *your handbag*
το πορτοφόλι **του** *his wallet*
οι αποσκευές **τους** *their luggage*

Here is the full list of possessive adjectives:

μου	moo	*my*	μας	mas	*our*
σου	soo	*your* (familiar)	σας	sas	*your* (formal)
του	too	*his*	τους	toos	*their*
της	tis	*her*			
του	too	*its*			

8 Verbs

(*a*) The most common categories of Greek verbs end in –ω, –ώ and –ομαι. The personal pronoun is not normally used because verbs are conjugated, i.e. each form has a different ending, and it is this *verb ending* that shows the subject of the verb.

πίνω	píno	*I drink*	πίνουμε	pínoome	*we drink*
πίνεις	pínis	*you drink*	πίνετε	pínete	*you drink*
πίνει	píni	*he, she, it drinks*	πίνουν	pínoon	*they drink*
μιλώ	miló	*I speak*	μιλούμε	miloóme	*we speak*
μιλάς	milás	*you speak*	μιλάτε	miláte	*you speak*
μιλάει	milái	*he, she, it speaks*	μιλούν	miloón	*they speak*
έρχομαι	érhome	*I come*	ερχόμαστε	erhómaste	*we come*
έρχεσαι	érhese	*you come*	έρχεστε	érheste	*you come*
έρχεται	érhete	*he, she, it comes*	έρχονται	érhonde	*they come*

(*b*) The auxiliary verbs έχω (*to have*) and είμαι (*to be*):

έχω	ého	*I have*	έχουμε	éhoome	*we have*
έχεις	éhis	*you have*	έχετε	éhete	*you have*
έχει	éhi	*he, she, it has*	έχουν	éhoon	*they have*
είμαι	íme	*I am*	είμαστε	ímaste	*we are*
είσαι	íse	*you are*	είστε	íste	*you are*
είναι	íne	*he, she, it is*	είναι	íne	*they are*

(*c*) There are a few Greek verbs, very commonly used, which are conjugated in an individual pattern. Examples among the verbs of this category used in the book:

πάω	páo	*I go*	πάμε	páme	*we go*
πας	pas	*you go*	πάτε	páte	*you go*
πάει	pái	*he, she, it goes*	πάνε	páne	*they go*

τρώω	tróo	*I eat*	τρώμε	tróme	*we eat*
τρως	tros	*you eat*	τρώτε	tróte	*you eat*
τρώει	trói	*he, she, it eats*	τρώνε	tróne	*they eat*

(*d*) It is quite common for a Greek verb to change substantially in a tense other than the present. Examples among the verbs of this category used in the book:

πίνω	píno	*I drink*	Τι θα πιείτε; ti tha pyíte
			What will you drink?
τρώω	tróo	*I eat*	Τι θα φάτε; ti tha fáte
			What will you eat?

έρχομαι   érhome   *I come*
έλα   éla   *come* (sing. imperative)
ελάτε   eláte   *come* (plural imperative)
    Έλα εδώ   *come here.*

(*e*) The verb **κάνω** (*I do, I make*) is often used in idiomatic expressions. Examples met in this book:

    Τι κάνεις; ti kánis   *How are you?*
    Κάνει ζέστη   káni zésti   *It is warm/hot.*
    Κάνει κρύο   káni krío   *It is cold.*
    Κάνω ένα ταξίδι   káno éna taksíthi   *I am going on a journey.*

(*f*) The English verb *I like* is expressed by the idiomatic Greek expression:

    μ' αρέσει   marési   *I like* (sing.)
    μ' αρέσουν   marésoon   *I like* (plural)

    Μ' αρέσει το κρασί.   marési to krasí   *I like the wine.*
    Μ' αρέσουν τα σταφύλια.   marésoon ta stafílya   *I like grapes.*
    Σ' αρέσει η Ελλάδα; sarési i elátha   *Do you like Greece?*
    Σ' αρέσουν τα βιβλία; sarésoon ta vivlía   *Do you like books?*

Note that the noun following the expression **μ' αρέσει**, *μ' αρέσουν*, etc., should be preceded by its *definite* article.

(g) Asking and answering questions

There are two ways of asking a question in Greek. Often the speaker merely raises his voice at the end of the sentence:

> Θέλετε ένα καφέ; thélete éna kafé *Do you want a coffee?*
> Έχετε τίποτα να δηλώσετε; éhete típota na thilósete *Do you have anything to declare?*

or he can reverse the order of the subject and the verb:

> Ο Γιάννης **θέλει** ένα καφέ. o yánis théli éna kafé *John wants a coffee.* (statement)
> **Θέλει** ο Γιάννης ένα καφέ; théli o yánis éna kafé *Does John want a coffee?* (question)

You give an affirmative answer using the same order of words (subject-verb) as in English:

> Ναι, θέλω ένα καφέ. ne thélo éna kafé *Yes, I want a coffee.*
> Ναι, ο Γιάννης θέλει ένα καφέ. ne o yánis théli éna kafé *Yes, John wants a coffee.*

or you give a negative answer adding **δεν** *(not)* before the verb:

> Όχι, **δεν** θέλω ένα καφέ. óhi **then** thélo éna kafé *No, I do not want a coffee.*
> Όχι, ο Γιάννης **δεν** θέλει ένα καφέ. óhi o yánis **then** théli éna kafé *No, John does not want a coffee.*

Some of the most common question words in Greek are:

τι; *what?*
> Τι θέλετε; ti thélete *What do you want?*

πως; *how?*
> Πως είστε; pos íste *How are you?*

που; *where?*
> Που είναι το ούζο; poo íne to oózo *Where is the ouzo?*

ποιός (masc.)
ποιά (fem.) } *who? which?*
ποιό (neut.)

ποιός είναι ο κύριος Σμίθ;
pyós íne o kírios smíth
Who is Mr Smith?
ποιό κρασί προτιμάτε;
pyó krasí protimáte
Which wine do you prefer?

πόσο; *how much?*
πόσο κάνει; póso káni   *How much does it cost?*
πόσο ούζο θέλετε;   póso oózo thélete   *How much ouzo do you want?*

Compare:

ΑΚΡΟΠΟΛΙΣ	**ΤΑΞΙ**	**ΟΛΥΜΠΙΑ**
AKROPOLIS	TAXI	OLYMPIA

Practise the Greek letters

What are the names of these popular Greek islands?

1 **ΚΡΗΤΗ**
2 **ΜΥΚΟΝΟΣ**
3 **ΡΟΔΟΣ**
4 **ΣΑΜΟΣ**
5 **ΚΕΡΚΥΡΑ**
6 **ΑΙΓΙΝΑ**

1 General Expressions

a. Yes, No **b.** Hello, Goodbye **c.** Please, Thank you **d.** Mr, Mrs **e.** The **f.** I, You, My, Your

a. ναι ne *yes*
όχι óhi *no*

Ναι, παρακαλώ ne parakaló	*Yes, please.*
Όχι, ευχαριστώ óhi efharistó	*No, thank you.*
Εντάξει. endáksi	*All right.*

b. Γειά σου yásoo *hello/goodbye* (informal)
Χαίρετε hérete *hello/goodbye* (formal)
Καλημέρα Kaliméra *good morning*
Καλησπέρα Kalispéra *good evening*
Καληνύχτα Kalinihta *good night*
Αντίο andío *goodbye*

Τι κάνεις; ti kánis	*How are you?* (informal)
Μιά χαρά, εσύ; myá hará esí	*Fine, and you?*
Τι κάνετε; ti kánete	*How are you?* (formal)
Πολύ καλά, εσείς; polí kalá esís	*Very well, and you?*

c. Ευχαριστώ efharistó *Thank you*
Παρακαλώ parakaló *Don't mention it*

Ευχαριστώ πολύ! efharistó polí	*Thank you very much!*

d. κύριος   kírios   *Mr*
   κυρία   kiría   *Mrs*
   δεσποινίς   **the**spinís   *Miss*

Καλημέρα, κύριε! kaliméra kírie	*Good morning, Sir!*
Ευχαριστώ, κυρία! efharistó kiría	*Thank you, Madam!*
Με συγχωρείτε, δεσποινίς!	*Excuse me, Miss*
me sinhoríte **the**spinís	
Είμαι ο κύριος Νότας	*I am Mr Notas*
íme o kírios Nótas	
Είμαι η κυρία Νότα	*I am Mrs Notas*
íme i kiría Nóta	

e. ο, η, το,   o, i, to   *the (m., f., n.)*
   οι, οι, τα   i, i, ta   *the (plural)*
   ένας, μία, ένα   énas, mía, éna   *a, an*
   αυτός, αυτή, αυτό   aftós, aftí, aftó   *this*

ο χάρτης o hártis	*the map*
αυτός ο χάρτης aftós o hártis	*this map*
η τσάντα i tsánta	*the handbag*
αυτή η τσάντα aftí i tsánta	*this handbag*
Μ' αρέσει αυτό. marési aftó	*I like this (one).*

f. εσείς   esís   *you (formal)*
   εγώ   eghó   *I*
   ο . . . μου   o . . . moo   *my (m.)*
   η . . . μου   i . . . moo   *my (f.)*
   το . . . μου   to . . . moo   *my (n.)*
   ο . . . σας   o . . . sas   *your (formal m.)*
   η . . . σας   i . . . sas   *your (formal f.)*
   το . . . σας   to . . . sas   *your (formal n.)*

ο άντρας μου o ándras moo	*my husband*
η γυναίκα μου i yinéka moo	*my wife*
Το διαβατήριο σας, παρακαλώ	*Your passport, please*
to **thi**avatírio sas parakaló	
Ορίστε! oríste	*Here you are!*
Είναι αυτή η βαλίτσα σας;	*Is this your suitcase?*
íne aftí i valítsa sas	
Ναι, ευχαριστώ! né efharistó	*Yes, thank you.*
Όχι, αυτή δεν είναι η βαλίτσα μου.	*No, this is not my*
óhi aftí then íne i valítsa moo	*suitcase.*

1 General Expressions

1 You want to say *hello* to a Greek. What do you say?

2 Someone asks you: **Τι κάνετε;** What do you answer?

3 You want to say *goodbye*. What do you say?

4 You want to say *good evening*. What do you say?

Someone offers you an orange.

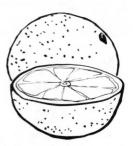

5 You want to accept. What do you say?

6 If you want to refuse, what do you say?

7 The policeman wants to see your passport. What does he say?

8 The policeman wants to know your name. Your name is Mrs Smith. What do you say?

The customs officer wants to know
if this is your suitcase.

9 If the suitcase belongs to you, what do you say?

10 If the suitcase does not belong to you, what do you say?

11 You want to apologise to someone. What do you say?

- In Greece, you usually address a man as **κύριε**, a married
  woman as **κυρία** and an unmarried woman as **δεσποινίς**:
  Καλημέρα **κύριε** Σμιθ
  Καλησπέρα **κυρία** Σμιθ
  Με συγχωρείτε **δεσποινίς**!

- When being introduced, you say **χαίρω πολύ** (*pleased to
  meet you*):
  Είμαι ο Γιάννης
  Χαίρω πολύ, Γιάννη
  Note that the final letter -s of a Greek name is usually left
  out when speaking to the person directly:
  Γειά σου Πέτρο (though his name is Πέτρος)
  Τι κάνεις Νίκο; (though his name is Νίκος)

- When a man's surname ends in -s, his wife uses the name
  without its final -s:
  ο κύριος Παυλάκης   *but* η κυρία Παυλάκη.
  ο κύριος Νότας   *but* η κυρία Νότα
  If a husband's surname ends in -os, his wife's surname ends
  in -ου:
  ο κύριος Σταυράκος   *but* η κυρία Σταυράκου

- When asking *How are you?* you would say **τι κάνεις**; to
  someone you know well, but **τι κάνετε**; to someone you
  have just met:
  Τι κάνεις Μαρία; **Τι κάνετε** κυρία Πήτερσον;
  The reply could be:
  μια χαρά   (*fine*); [πολύ]καλά   ([*very*]*well*);
  έτσι κι έτσι   (*so-so*).

- When you want to say *Excuse me* you can either say **με
  συγχωρείτε** or **συγγνώμη**:
  με συγχωρείτε κύριε Παυλάκη
  συγγνώμη Μαρία

Arriving in Greece 2

a. Customs **b.** Papers **c.** Nationality

a. ΤΕΛΩΝΕΙΟ τελωνείο telonío *customs*
ΤΕΛΩΝΕΙΑΚΟΣ ΕΛΕΓΧΟΣ *customs inspection*
  teloniakós élenhos
ΕΙΔΗ ΓΙΑ ΔΗΛΩΣΗ *goods to declare*
  íthi ya thílosi
ΤΙΠΟΤΑ ΓΙΑ ΔΗΛΩΣΗ *nothing to declare*
  típota ya thílosi
αποσκευές aposkevés *luggage*
βαλίτσα valítsa *suitcase*
τσάντα tsánta *handbag*
πορτ-μπαγκάζ port-bagáz *boot (of a car)*

Ανοίξτε τη βαλίτσα, παρακαλώ. aníkste ti valítsa parakaló	*Open the suitcase please*

Έχετε να δηλώσετε τίποτα;
  éhete na thilósete típota
	*Do you have anything
	  to declare?*

Όχι, δεν έχω να δηλώσω τίποτα.
  óhi then ého na thilóso típota
	*No, I have nothing to
	  declare.*

Αυτό είναι για προσωπική χρήση.
  aftó íne ya prosopikí hrísi
	*This is for my
	  personal use.*

καλό ταξίδι! kaló taksíthi	*Have a pleasant trip!*

b. διαβατήριο thiavatírio *passport*
τα χαρτιά ta hartiá *car registration papers*
άδεια οδηγήσεως áthia othiyíseos *driving licence*
όνομα ónoma *name*
διεύθυνση thiéfthinsi *address*
ημερομηνία imerominía *date*
υπογραφή ipoghrafí *signature*

ΕΛΕΓΧΟΣ ΔΙΑΒΑΤΗΡΙΟΥ élenhos thiavatiríoo	*passport control*
Το διαβατήριο σας, παρακαλώ. to thiavatírio sas parakaló	*Your passport, please.*
Πως σας λένε; pos sas léne	*What is your name?*
Με λένε ... me léne	*My name is . . .*

είστε εδώ για δουλειά;
  íste ethó ya thoolyá
	*Are you here on
	  business?*

Όχι, είμαι εδώ για διακοπές.
  óhi íme ethó ya thiakopés
	*No, I am here on
	  holiday.*

c. υπηκοότητα ipikoótita — *nationality*
ΕΛΛΑΔΑ Ελλάδα elátha — *Greece*
Έλληνας élinas — *Greek (man)*
Ελληνίδα elinítha — *Greek (woman)*
Ελληνικά eliniká — *Greek (language)*
ΑΛΛΟΔΑΠΟΙ αλλοδαποί alothapí — *foreigners*
Μεγάλη Βρετανία megháli vretanía — *Great Britain*
ΑΓΓΛΙΑ Αγγλία anglía — *England*
Άγγλος ánglos — *English (man)*
Αγγλίδα anglítha — *English (woman)*
Αγγλικά angliká — *English (language)*
ΑΜΕΡΙΚΗ Αμερική amerikí — *America (USA)*
Αμερικάνος amerikános — *American (man)*
Αμερικανίδα amerikanítha — *American (woman)*
ΑΥΣΤΡΑΛΙΑ Αυστραλία afstralía — *Australia*
Αυστραλός afstralós — *Australian (man)*
Αυστραλέζα afstraléza — *Australian (woman)*
Ουαλλία ooalía — *Wales*
Ουαλλός ooalós — *Welsh (man)*
Ουαλλέζα ooaléza — *Welsh (woman)*
Σκωτία skotía — *Scotland*
Σκωτσέζος skotsézos — *Scottish (man)*
Σκωτσέζα skotséza — *Scottish (woman)*
ΠΡΟΞΕΝΕΙΟ προξενείο proksenío — *consulate*
ΑΓΓΛΙΚΗ ΠΡΕΣΒΕΙΑ — *British Embassy*
Αγγλική Πρεσβεία anglikí presvía

Είστε Άγγλος; íste ánglos — *Are you English?*
Ναί, είμαι Αγγλος ne íme ánglos — *Yes, I am English.*
Μιλάτε Αγγλικά; miláte angliká — *Do you speak English?*
Ναι, μιλώ Αγγλικά. ne miló angliká — *Yes, I speak English.*
Όχι, δεν μιλώ Αγγλικά. — *No, I do not speak*
óhi then miló angliká — *English.*
Έχετε μία αγγλική εφημερίδα; — *Do you have an English*
éhete mía anglikí efimerítha — *newspaper?*
Έχετε αγγλικά περιοδικά; — *Do you have any*
éhete angliká periothiká — *English magazines?*
... στην Ελλάδα stin elátha — *in Greece*

2 Arriving in Greece

What are these called in Greek?

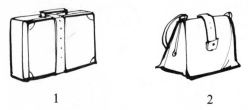

1   2

3 You arrive in Greece and have to go through the passport control. Which sign should you look for?

4 The policeman wants to see your passport. What does he say?

5 He asks you your name. What do you say?

6 He asks you if you are English. If you are English, what do you answer?

7 You get to customs. Which exit should you take if you have nothing to declare?

8 The customs officer stops you and asks you to open your suitcase. What does he say?

9 After the customs inspection, he wishes you a pleasant trip. What does he say?

What are these countries called in Greek?

10

11

12

13 You want to buy an English newspaper. What do you ask at the news-stand?

- The address of the **British Embassy** in Athens is:
  1 Ploutarchou St, Athens (Tel: 723-6211/9)

- Other useful addresses:
  Aliens Bureau: 9 Halkokondili St (1st floor)
  Athens (Tel: 362-8301)
  Main Tourist Police Office: 7 Singrou Avenue
  Athens (Tel: 923-9224)
  Y.M.C.A. Youth Hostels (maximum stay is 10 days)
  at: 11 Amerikis St, in Athens (Tel: 362-4294)
  11 Agias Sofias St, in Thessaloniki
  (Tel: 031-276-1440)
  Timios Stavros quarter, at Rethymnon (Crete)
  (Tel: 0831-23324)
  British High Commission (in Cyprus):
  Alexander Pallis St, Nikosia (Tel: 923-9224)

- If you are **driving in Greece**, you need to carry with you a valid British driving licence, or an international driving permit.

- Cars and motorcycles can be hired from agencies. Prices vary according to season, type of car and length of time required.

- Chartering of vessels for pleasure trips or tourist cruises is permissible only in the cases of vessels flying the Greek flag, formally recognized as professional tourist craft.

- The export of Greek **antiquities** is forbidden. Exceptions are granted by the Archaelogical Office (13 Polignotou St) which issues permits.

- The daily newspaper *The Athens News* is printed in English.

---

3 Driving a Car

a. Cars **b.** Roads **c.** Service Stations
d. Parking

a. αυτοκίνητο aftokínito — *car*
τροχόσπιτο trohóspito — *caravan*
φορτηγό fortighó — *lorry*
οδική κυκλοφορία othikí kikloforía — *traffic*
οδηγός othigós — *driver*
ταχύτητα tahítita — *speed*

Ενοικιάσεις αυτοκινήτων enikyásis afrokiníton	*car hire*
Θέλω να νοικιάσω ένα αυτοκίνητο Thélo na nikyáso éna aftokínito	*I would like to hire a car*

b. δρόμος thrómos — *road*
εθνική οδός ethnikí othós — *motorway*
μονόδρομος monóthromos — *one-way traffic*
ΔΙΟΔΙΑ διόδια thióthia — *toll*
παράκαμψη parákampsi — *diversion*

ΑΠΑΓΟΡΕΥΕΤΑΙ Η ΕΙΣΟΔΟΣ apaghorévete i ísothos	*No entry*
ΑΠΑΓΟΡΕΥΕΤΑΙ ΤΟ ΠΡΟΣΠΕΡΑΣΜΑ apaghorévete to prospérasma	*No overtaking*
ΑΔΙΕΞΟΔΟΣ athiéksothos	*No through road*
Προσοχή! prosohí	*Caution!*

c. πρατήριο βενζίνης pratírio venzínis — *petrol station*
βενζίνη venzíni — *petrol*
απλή/σούπερ aplí/soóper — *2 star/4 star*
λάδι láthi — *oil*
νερό neró — *water*
ντήζελ dízel — *diesel*

Πόση βενζίνη θέλετε; pósi venzíni thélete	*How much petrol do you want?*
Γεμάτο! yemáto	*Fill it up!*
Ελέγξτε το λάδι, παρακαλώ. elénkste to láthi, parakaló	*Check the oil, please.*

d. ΠΑΡΚΙΝΓΚ párkin — *parking, car park*
παρκόμετρο parkómetro — *parking meter*

ΑΠΑΓΟΡΕΥΕΤΑΙ Η ΣΤΑΘΜΕΥΣΗ apaghorévete i státhmefsi	*No parking.*

Car breakdown, Accidents → 20

3 Driving a Car

What are these called in Greek?

1   2

You stop your car at a service station to buy petrol.

3 The attendant wants to know how much petrol you want.
   What does he ask?

4 You want the tank filled up. What do you say?

5 How do you ask him to check the oil?

Explain in Greek what the following signs mean:

6   7   8

Look at these two signs:

9 Which sign indicates that you are approaching a toll post?

10 Which sign indicates that you are approaching Customs?

- **Traffic regulations and signals** are generally similar to those of other European countries. Seat-belts must be worn by the driver and front-seat passenger. Note that special care should be taken in Greece when negotiating unguarded railway level-crossings.

- **Breakdown Service:** ELPA's road assistance service can be reached by dialling 104. This service functions on a 24-hour basis every day in Athens and Thessaloniki and from 7 am to 10 pm in most of the other towns. Note that foreign motorists who are members of national Automobile or Touring Clubs in their own country are granted free road assistance just like ELPA's Greek members.

- **Speed limits:**   50 km/hour within a town (31 mph)
                       100 km/hour outside a town (62 mph)

- There are **toll gates** on the two motorways, one leading to Northern Greece and the other to the Peloponnese. The charges are very low.

- **Parking** in Athens is quite difficult, though several parking areas are reserved for tourists. Police are entitled to impose and collect fines on the spot.

4 Finding Your Way

a. Maps **b.** In Town **c.** Streets **d.** Directions

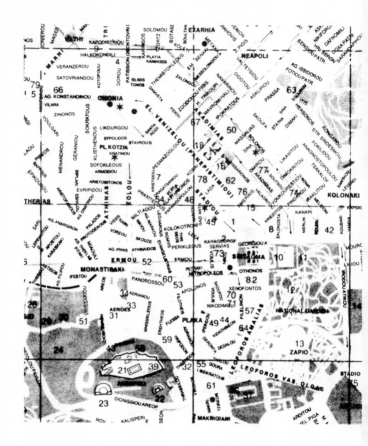

a. χάρτης hártis   *map, road map*

χάρτης της Ελλάδας hártis tis eláthas	*map of Greece*
οδικός χάρτης othikós hártis	*street map*
Ένα χάρτη της πόλης, παρακαλώ éna hárti tis pólis parakaló	*A city map, please*

b. ΠΟΛΗ πόλη póli — *city, town*
 ΚΕΝΤΡΟ κέντρο kéndro — *town centre*
 ΑΡΧΑΙΑ arhéa — *old*
 ΝΕΑ néa — *new*

ΑΡΧΑΙΑ ΚΟΡΙΝΘΟΣ arhéa kórinthos	*Old Corinth*
ΝΕΑ ΜΑΚΡΗ néa mákri	*New Makri*
Που μένετε; poo ménete	*Where do you live/are staying?*
Μένω στην Αθήνα. méno stin athína	*I live/am staying in Athens.*

c. ΟΔΟΣ οδός othós — *street*
 ΛΕΩΦΟΡΟΣ λεωφόρος leofóros — *avenue*
 ΠΛΑΤΕΙΑ πλατεία platía — *square*
 ΠΕΖΟΔΡΟΜΟΣ pezóthromos — *pedestrian zone*
 φανάρι fanári — *traffic light*

ΟΔΟΣ ΑΘΗΝΑΣ othós athinás	*Athens Street*
Σύνταγμα síntagma	*Sintagma Square (in Athens)*
Ομόνοια omónia	*Omonia Square (in Athens)*

d. Που είναι...; poo íne — *Where is...?*
 εδώ ethó — *here*
 εκεί ekí — *there*
 στρίψετε δεξιά strípsete theksyá — *turn right*
 στρίψετε αριστερά strípsete aristerá — *turn left*
 πηγαίνετε ευθεία piyénete efthía — *go straight ahead*
 στη γωνία sti ghonía — *at the corner*

Που είναι η στάση; poo íne i stási	*Where is the bus-stop?*
Πως μπορώ να πάω στο...; pos boró na páo sto	*How do I get to...?*
Ευθεία, στο δεύτερο στενό δεξιά. efthía sto théftero stenó theksyá	*Straight ahead, second turn to the right.*
Είναι μακριά; íne makriá	*Is it far?*
Όχι, είναι αρκετά κοντά. óhi íne arketá kondá	*No, it is quite near.*

Distance → 7, Tourist Attractions → 15

4 Finding Your Way

1 You want to buy a road map of Greece. What do you say?

2 You want to buy a city map. What do you say?

3 You want to ask someone where Athens St. is. What do you say?

4 How do you tell someone to turn right?

Look at the road signs below.

In which direction must you turn (right, left, straight ahead)

5 When you want to go to Corinth?

6 When you want to go to Athens?

7 When you want to go to Loutraki?

8 You don't know where the bus stop is. How do you ask a passerby?

9 You want to know if it is far. What do you say?

10 Someone tells you that it is straight ahead, second turn to the right. What does he say?

11 Say the names of these major Greek cities (the cities are listed in geographical order from north to south):
ΘΕΣΣΑΛΟΝΙΚΗ, ΑΛΕΞΑΝΔΡΟΥΠΟΛΗ, ΛΑΡΙΣΑ,
ΛΑΜΙΑ, ΛΙΒΑΔΕΙΑ, ΑΘΗΝΑ, ΚΟΡΙΝΘΟΣ, ΠΑΤΡΑ,
ΑΡΓΟΣ, ΤΡΙΠΟΛΗ, ΚΑΛΑΜΑΤΑ.

- **Maps**, brochures, lists of hotels and other useful information can be obtained from the local tourist offices which are in most main tourist resorts.

- **Street signs** in central areas are usually written in both Greek and Latin letters.

- The **traffic light** sequence is: red (stop), green (go), yellow (caution), red (stop).

- Useful **road signs**, though not very common in Greece, are:

ΑΝΩΜΑΛΙΑ ΟΔΟΣΤΡΩΜΑΤΟΣ	*Uneven road surface*
ΕΡΓΑ ΕΠΙ ΤΗΣ ΟΔΟΥ	*Roadworks in progress*
ΟΛΙΣΘΗΡΟ ΟΔΟΣΤΡΩΜΑ	*Slippery road surface*
ΠΟΡΕΙΑ ΥΠΟΧΡΕΩΤΙΚΗ ΔΕΞΙΑ	*Keep right*
ΔΙΑΒΑΣΗ ΠΕΖΩΝ	*Pedestrian crossing*

5 Public Transport

a. Railways **b.** Aeroplanes **c.** Ships
d. Transport **e.** Information

a. σιδηρόδρομος si**th**iró**th**romos — *railway*
αποβάθρα apováthra — *platform*
σταθμός stathmós — *station*
γραφείο αποσκευών — *left-luggage office*
  ghrafío aposkevón
γραμμή ghramí — *track*
τραίνο tréno — *train*
ΤΑΧΕΙΑ ταχεία tahía — *express train*
ΑΥΤΟΚΙΝΗΤΑΜΑΞΑ — *(railway) coach*
  αυτοκινητάμαξα aftokinitámaksa
ΚΛΙΝΑΜΑΞΑ κλινάμαξα — *sleeping car*
  klinámaksa
Αχθοφόρε! ahthofóre — *Porter!*
Μπορείτε να με βοηθήσετε; — *Can you help me?*
  boríte na me voithísete

b. αερολιμένας aeroliménas — *airport (formal Greek)*
αεροδρόμιο aerothrómio — *airport (colloquial)*
αίθουσα αναμονής — *waiting-room*
  éthousa anamonís
ΓΡΑΜΜΕΣ ΕΞΩΤΕΡΙΚΟΥ — *international departures*
  ghramés eksoterikoó

| ΠΤΗΣΗ πτήση ptísi | *flight* |
| ΟΛΥΜΠΙΑΚΗ ΑΕΡΟΠΟΡΙΑ
Olimbiakí aeroporía | *OLYMPIC AIRWAYS* |

c.

βαπόρι vapóri	*steamer*
καράβι karávi	*boat*
φεριμπότ ferimbót	*ferry*
ΛΙΜΗΝ λιμήν limín	*harbour* (formal Greek)
λιμάνι limáni	*harbour* (colloquial)

ΚΕΝΤΡΙΚΟΣ ΛΙΜΗΝ ΠΕΙΡΑΙΩΣ kendrikós limín pireós	*central harbour of Piraeus*
Τι ώρα φεύγει; ti óra févghi	*What time does it leave?*
Το καράβι για την Αίγινα to karávi ya tin éghina	*The boat to Aegina*
Τι ώρα φτάνει; ti óra ftáni	*What time does it arrive?*

d.

λεωφορείο leoforío	*bus*
ΣΤΑΣΗ στάση stási	*bus stop*
ΕΙΣΟΔΟΣ ísothos	*entrance*
ΕΞΟΔΟΣ éksothos	*exit*
ΤΑΞΙ ταξί taksí	*taxi*

ΣΤΑΘΜΟΣ ΤΑΞΙ stathmós taksí	*taxi stand*
Καλέστε μου ένα ταξί. kaléste moo éna taksí	*Get me a taxi.*
Στήν Ομόνοια, παρακαλώ. stin omónia parakaló	*To Omonia Square, please.*

e.

ΠΛΗΡΟΦΟΡΙΕΣ plirofories	*information*
ΔΡΟΜΟΛΟΓΙΑ thromológhia	*timetables*
ΠΡΟΕΛΕΥΣΗ proélefsi	*origin*
ΠΡΟΟΡΙΣΜΟΣ proorismós	*destination*
ΑΦΙΞΕΙΣ afíksis	*arrival* (*times*)
ΑΝΑΧΩΡΗΣΕΙΣ anahorísis	*departure* (*times*)
ΕΙΣΙΤΗΡΙΑ isitíria	*tickets*
ΘΕΣΗ thési	*seat*

| Ένα εισιτήριο για την Αθήνα.
éna isitírio ya tin athína | *A ticket to Athens.* |
| Ένα εισιτήριο με επιστροφή.
éna isitírio me epistrofí | *A return ticket.* |

Luggage → 2, Time → 8, Money → 9

5 Public Transport

OLYMPIC AIRWAYS

1 You want to go to the airport. What do you say to the taxi driver?

2 You are at the airport and want to find the information desk. Which sign must you look for?

3 You want to go to Departures. Do you follow the sign on the right (δεξιά) or on the left (αριστερά)?

4 What do you call a ship which can take you and your car, for example, from Italy to Greece?

5 What do you call this kind of boat?

6 Look at this Athens subway ticket. The traveller got on at ΘΗΣΕΙΟ. Where did the traveller go?

7 You want to get on the bus. Which door do you use? The one with the sign ΕΙΣΟΔΟΣ or the sign ΕΞΟΔΟΣ?

You are at the railway station.

8 Tell the ticket clerk you would like a ticket to Athens.

9 Ask for a return ticket.

- **Athens airport** (Eliniko Airport) has two terminals. The new building to the east (East Airport) serves the foreign airlines and the buildings to the west (West Airport) serve only Olympic Airways. Tell the taxi driver in Athens which terminal you want because the approaches are different.

- There are two **railway stations** in Athens. Trains leaving from the main station ΚΕΝΤΡΙΚΟΣ ΣΤΑΘΜΟΣ (or Larissa Railway Station) go to Thessaly, Northern Greece and middle Europe. The narrow-gauge railway at the Peloponnesus Station (Peloponnese Railway Station) goes south to Patras, Tripolis, Kalamata, etc. It takes about 5 minutes to walk between the two stations. You can buy first- and second-class tickets at considerably reduced rates for students and groups of more than ten persons. Note that the rail network is not very extensive in Greece. On the whole, bus connections are far more frequent and much faster than trains.

- There are two **bus terminals** in Athens. The buses to the Peloponnese leave from 100 Kifissoú St. Those going north (to Delphi, Larissa, Thebes, etc.) leave from 260 Liossíon St.

- **Taxis** are relatively cheap but they charge a supplement from the airport, railway station, harbour and for each piece of luggage.

6 Accommodation

a. Hotels, Camping **b.** Hotel Rooms
c. Prices **d.** Toilets

a. ΞΕΝΟΔΟΧΕΙΟ ksenothohío   *hotel*
   ΗΟΤΕΛ hotel   *hotel*
   ΚΑΜΠΙΝΓΚ camping   *campsite*
   ΞΕΝΩΝΑΣ ΝΕΟΤΗΤΑΣ   *youth hostel*
    ksenónas neótitas

Υπάρχει ένα ξενοδοχείο εδώ κοντά;	*Is there an hotel near*
ipárhi éna ksenothohío ethó kondá	*here?*
Που είναι το κάμπινγκ;	*Where is the campsite?*
poo íne to "camping"	

b.

δωμάτιο	thomátio	*room*
κρεβάτι	kreváti	*bed*
μπάνιο	bánio	*bath*
ντους	doos	*shower*
κλειδί	klithí	*key*
ασανσέρ	asansér	*lift*
όροφος	órofos	*floor*
ισόγειο (ΙΣ)	isóyio	*ground floor*

Έχετε ένα δωμάτιο, παρακαλώ; éhete éna **tho**mátio parakaló	*Have you got a vacant room please?*
μονό δωμάτιο monó **tho**matio	*single room*
διπλό δωμάτιο thipló **tho**mátio	*double room*
Για πόσα άτομα; ya pósa átoma	*For how many people?*
Δωμάτιο με ντους **tho**mátio me doos	*A room with a shower.*
Έχω κρατήσει ένα δωμάτιο ého kratísi éna **tho**mátio	*I have booked a room*
Για πόσες μέρες; ya póses méres	*For how many days?*
για μία νύχτα ya mía nihta	*for one night*
για δύο νύχτες ya **th**ío nihtes	*for two nights*
Όλα πιασμένα. óla pyasména	*There's no vacancy.*

c.

ΤΙΜΗ τιμή timí	*price*
ΛΟΓΑΡΙΑΣΜΟΣ λογαριασμός logharyazmós	*bill*

ΤΙΜΗ ΔΩΜΑΤΙΟΥ Τιμή δωματίου timí **tho**matíoo	*price of the room*
Πόσο κοστίζει αυτό; póso kostízi aftó	*How much does it cost?*
...με πρόγευμα me próyevma	*...with breakfast*
Θέλω να πληρώσω thélo na pliróso	*I'd like to pay*

d.

τουαλέττα tooaléta	*toilet*
ΑΝΔΡΩΝ an**th**rón	*MEN's*
ΓΥΝΑΙΚΩΝ yinekón	*WOMEN's*

Που είναι η τουαλέττα; poo íne i tooaléta	*Where is the toilet?*
Εκεί πέρα, στα αριστερά. ekí péra sta aristerá	*Over there, to the left.*

Luggage → 2, Money → 9

6 Accommodation

What are these called in Greek?

1

2

3 You are looking for a hotel. What do you ask a passerby?

4 How do you ask at the reception desk if they have a vacancy?

5 You want a room with a shower. What do you say?

6 You want to know how much the room costs. What do you say?

7 The receptionist tells you the price of the room. What is the *price of the room* in Greek?

8 You are in the lift and want to go to the ground floor. Which button do you push?

9 You want to leave and pay for the room. What do you say to the receptionist?

10 You are looking for the toilet. How do you ask where it is?

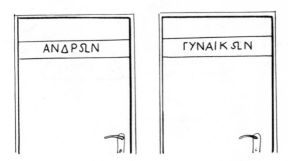

11 Which word is on the door of the men's room?

12 Which word is on the door of the women's room?

- Depending on the visitor's preferences and on what he is prepared to spend, there is a choice of **hotels** from luxury- to fifth-class category, service flats, rooms in private houses and official campsites. Room **prices** at hotels are usually displayed on the backs of bedroom doors and at Reception, along with breakfast and service charges. All visitors are required to fill in a registration form on arrival.

- **Reservations** can be made by writing directly to the hotel or with the Head Office of the Hotel Chamber at 6 Aristidou St in Athens (Tel. 323-350I)

- **Camping.** You should only camp at official campsites. There are campsites in some of the most picturesque parts of the country. All campsites have lavatory facilities, drinking-water and electricity. Information on locations and on the detailed amenities offered in each campsite can be obtained by the Tourist Office.

- **Pre-season** is from April 1 to May 15, **peak season** from May 16 to October 15, **after-season** from October 16 to October 30.

- The **voltage** in Greece is generally 220 volts.

7 Numbers, Weights and Measures

a. Numbers   b. Weights and Measures

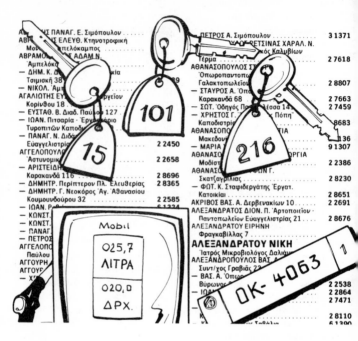

a.

0 μηδεν **mithén**	15 δεκα-πέντε **thekapénde**
1 ένα **éna**	16 δεκα-έξι **thekaéksi**
2 δύο **thío**	17 δεκα-εφτά **thekaeftá**
3 τρία **tría**	18 δεκα-οχτώ **thekaohtó**
4 τέσσερα **tésera**	19 δεκα-εννιά **thekaenyá**
5 πέντε **pénde**	20 είκοσι **íkosi**
6 έξι **éksi**	21 είκοσι ένα **ikosiéna**
7 εφτά **eftá**	22 είκοσι δύο **ikosithío**
8 οχτώ **ohtó**	30 τριάντα **triánda**
9 εννιά **enyá**	40 σαράντα **saránda**
10 δέκα **théka**	50 πενήντα **peninda**
11 έν-δεκα **éntheka**	60 εξήντα **eksínda**
12 δώ-δεκα **thótheka**	70 εβδομήντα **evthomínda**
13 δεκα-τρία **thekatría**	80 ογδόντα **oghthónda**
14 δεκα-τέσσερα **thekatésera**	90 ενενήντα **eneninda**

100 εκατό	ekató	400 τετρακόσια	tetrakósia
101 εκατον ένα	ekatón éna	500 πεντακόσια	pendakósia
102 εκατό δύο	ekató thío	600 εξακόσια	eksakósia
150 εκατό πενήντα	ekató penínda	700 εφτακόσια	eftakósia
200 διακόσια	thiakósia	800 οχτακόσια	ohtakósia
300 τριακόσια	triakósia	900 εννιακόσια	enyakósia

1 000 χίλια	hília	
1 500 χίλια πεντακόσια	hília pendakósia	
2 000 δύο χιλιάδες	thío hiliáthes	
3 000 τρεις χιλιάδες	trís hiliáthes	
4 000 τέσσερις χιλιάδες	téseris hiliáthes	
10 000 δέκα χιλιάδες	théka hiliáthes	
100 000 εκατό χιλιάδες	ekató hiliáthes	
1 000 000 ένα εκατομμύριο	éna ekatomírio	

διακόσιες δραχμές **thiakósies thrahmés**	*two hundred drachmas*
χίλιες δραχμές **hílies thrahmés**	*a thousand drachmas*

b.

αριθμός	arithmós	*number*
ΚΙΛΟ κιλό	kiló	*kilo*
ΛΙΤΡΟ λίτρο	lítro	*litre*
μέτρο	métro	*metre*
χιλιόμετρο	hilyómetro	*kilometre*
πόσο;	póso	*how much?*
πόσα;	pósa	*how many?*
πολύ	polí	*a lot*
λίγο	lígho	*a little*
περισσότερο	perisótero	*more*
λιγότερο	lighótero	*less*

ένα κιλό ντομάτες **éna kiló domátes**	*a kilo of tomatoes*
τρία κιλά μήλα **tría kilá míla**	*three kilos of apples*
ένα λίτρο νερό **éna lítro neró**	*a litre of water*
διακόσια μέτρα από το σταθμό **thiakósia métra apó to stathmó**	*200 metres from the station*
πενήντα χιλιόμετρα για την Αθήνα **penínda hilyómetra ya tin athína**	*50 kilometres to Athens*

Time, Dates → 8

7 Numbers, Weights and Measures

In which rooms are the hotel guests staying?

1 Mr Πετράκης

2 Mr Πέτσης

3 Mr Marshall

4 Mr Smith

Look at the picture below.

Say how much it costs to rent these things on the beach:

5 umbrella

6 deck-chair

7 sun-bed

8 canoe

9 pedal boat

10 Read the following distances in Greek:

ΑΘΗΝΑ–ΘΗΒΑ	72
–ΛΑΜΙΑ	215
–ΛΑΡΙΣΑ	356
–ΘΕΣΣΑΛΟΝΙΚΗ	508
–ΕΥΖΩΝΟΙ	550
–ΚΟΡΙΝΘΟΣ	83
–ΠΑΤΡΑ	213

11 You are going shopping. How do you ask for a kilo of tomatoes?

12 You want to buy 3 kilos of apples. What do you say?

13 You want to buy a litre of water. What do you say?

– Greeks use the decimal system. The most common weight is the kilo (= 1000 grams or 2.2 lbs):

    Ένα κιλό μήλα, παρακαλώ. *A kilo of apples, please.*
    Δύο κιλά μήλα, παρακαλώ. *Two kilos of apples, please.*

– For smaller quantities they use;

    μισό κιλό τυρί   *half a kilo of cheese*
    ένα τέταρτο   *a quarter of a kilo*
    εκατό γραμμάρια   *100 grams*

a. Telling the Time   **b.** Times of the Day
c. Week and Month

a. ρολόι rolói	clock, watch
ώρα óra	hour
λεπτό leptó	minute
στιγμή stighmi	moment

δέκα λεπτά **th**éka leptá	ten minutes
μία ώρα mía óra	one hour
μισή ώρα misí ora	half an hour
ένα τέταρτο éna tétarto	a quarter of an hour
Τι ώρα είναι; ti óra íne	What time is it?
Είναι μία íne mía	It's one (o'clock)
Είναι τρεις íne trís	It's three (o'clock)
Πότε; póte	When?
Στίς έξι stís éksi	At six (o'clock)
Το απόγευμα to apóyevma	in the afternoon
το βράδυ to vrá**th**i	in the evening
Μια στιγμή, παρακαλώ myá stighmí parakaló	Just a moment, please.

b. μέρα   méra — *day time*
πρωί   proí — *morning*
μεσημέρι   mesiméri — *noon, midday*
απόγευμα   apóyevma — *afternoon*
βράδυ   vráthi — *evening*
νύχτα   níhta — *night*
μεσάνυχτα   mesánihta — *midnight*
σήμερα   símera — *today*
χθες   hthés — *yesterday*
αύριο   ávrio — *tomorrow*
κάθε μέρα   káthe méra — *every day*

Πότε φεύγετε; póte févyete	*When are you leaving?*
Αύριο το πρωί στις οχτώ. ávrio to proí stis ohtó	*Tomorrow morning at 8.*
Τι ώρα φεύγει το τραίνο; ti óra févyi to tréno	*At what time does the train leave?*
Στις δέκα το πρωί. stis théka to proí	*At 10 in the morning.*
Φτάνει στις έξι το βράδυ. ftáni stis eksi to vrathi	*It arrives at 6 in the evening.*

c. χρόνος   hrónos — *time, year*
μήνας   mínas — *month*
εβδομάδα   evthomátha — *week*
Δευτέρα   theftéra — *Monday*
Τρίτη   tríti — *Tuesday*
Τετάρτη   tetárti — *Wednesday*
Πέμπτη   pémpti — *Thursday*
Παρασκευή   paraskeví — *Friday*
Σάββατο   sávato — *Saturday*
Κυριακή   kiriakí — *Sunday*

Την περασμένη εβδομάδα. tin perasméni evthomátha	*Last week.*
Την άλλη εβδομάδα. tin áli evthomátha	*Next week.*
Κλειστό την Δευτέρα. Klistó tin theftéra	*Closed on Monday.*
Πόσο καιρό παίρνει; póso keró pérni	*How long does it take?*

Public Transport → 5, Numbers → 7

8 Times and Dates

How do you say the following in Greek?

1 The time of day from sunrise to noon.

2 The time of day from noon till sunset.

3 The time of day when it is dark.

4 60 minutes (= ?)

5 24 hours.

6 7 days (= ?)

7 You want to know what time it is. What do you say?

Say what time it is for each of the clocks below:

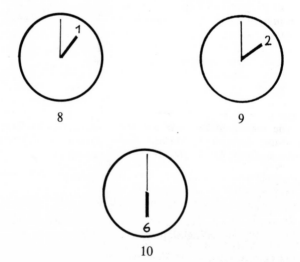

11 The hotel desk clerk wants to know when you are leaving. What does he ask you?

12 How do you answer that you are leaving tomorrow morning at 8 o'clock?

13 Read the airport departure times in Greek:

ΑΝΑΧΩΡΗΣΕΙΣ		
ΠΤΗΣΗ	ΠΡΟΟΡΙΣΜΟΣ	ΠΡΟΓΡΑΜΜΑΤΑ
OA 620	MYKONOS	9.05
OA 504	IRAKLION	10.10
OA 905	THESSALONIKI	11.20
OA 708	RODOS	12.00
OA 772	LIMNOS	12.45

14 How do you say in Greek:
  (a) in 20 minutes?
  (b) in half an hour?
  (c) in 10 days?
  (d) in 6 months?

- The **months of the year** are: Ιανουάριος, Φεβρουάριος, Μάρτιος, Απρίλιος, Μάϊος, Ιούνιος, Ιούλιος, Αύγουστος, Σεπτέμβριος, Οκτώβριος, Νοέμβριος, Δεκέμβριος.

- The **24-hour clock** is used for official purposes (on timetables, etc.)
  13.00 = 1 pm; 18.30 = 6.30 pm and so on.

- To say on Monday, on Tuesday, etc, you add **τη(ν)**, which is equivalent to the English preposition to:

  τη(ν) Δευτέρα   on Monday
  τη(ν) Τρίτη   on Tuesday and so on,
  but you should say:
  το Σάββατο   on Saturday

9 Money and Shopping

a. Money **b.** At the Bank, Changing Money
c. Shopping **d.** Paying

a. λεφτά leftá — *money*
κέρμα kérma — *coin*
ψιλά psilá — *small change*
ΔΡΑΧΜΗ δραχμή **th**rahmí — *drachma*

100 δραχμές ekató **th**rahmés	*100 drachmas*
5 000 δραχμές	*5 000 drachmas*
pénde hiliá**th**es **th**rahmés	
(ΔΡΧ.)	*(short for drachmas)*
έχετε καθόλου ψιλά;	*Have you got any*
éhete kathóloo psilá	*small change?*

b. ΤΡΑΠΕΖΑ τράπεζα trápeza — *bank*
ΣΥΝΑΛΛΑΓΜΑ συνάλλαγμα sinálagma — *currency exchange*
τράβελερς τσέκ trávelers tsek — *traveller's cheque*
πιστωτική κάρτα pistotikí kárta — *credit card*

Θέλω ν' αλλάξω ... thélo nalákso .. | *I'd like to change ...*
εκατό λίρες Αγγλίας | *one hundred pounds*
  ekató líres anglías
χίλια δολλάρια hília **tho**lária | *a thousand dollars*
Θέλω να εξαργυρώσω αυτό το τσέκ. | *I would like to cash*
  thélo na eksaryiróso aftó to tsek | *this cheque.*
Που να υπογράψω; | *Where should I sign?*
  poo na ipoghrápso

c. ΚΑΤΑΣΤΗΜΑ κατάστημα | *shop*
  katástima
ΑΓΟΡΑ αγορά aghorá | *market*
ΕΙΔΙΚΗ ΠΡΟΣΦΟΡΑ | *special offer*
  ειδική προσφορά ithikí prosforá
ΕΥΚΑΙΡΙΑ ευκαιρία efkería | *bargain*
ΑΝΟΙΚΤΟ aniktó | *open*
ΚΛΕΙΣΤΟ klistó | *closed*
ΣΥΡΑΤΕ sírate | *pull*
ΩΘΗΣΑΤΕ othísate | *push*

Τι θέλετε; ti thélete | *What would you like?*
Θέλω να δω πρώτα. | *I'm just looking*
  thélo na **thó** próta
Θέλω αυτό το βάζο. | *I'd like this vase.*
  thélo aftó to vázo
Θέλετε τίποτε άλλο; | *Would you like*
  thélece típote álo | *anything else?*
Όχι, ευχαριστώ óhi efharistó | *No, thank you.*

d. ΤΙΜΗ τιμή timí | *price*
ακριβό akrivó | *expensive*
φτηνό ftinó | *cheap*
δωρεάν thoreán | *free*
ΤΑΜΕΙΟ ταμείο tamío | *cashier/cash desk*

Πόσο κοστίζει αυτό; | *How much does*
  póso kostízi aftó | *this cost?*
Χίλιες Δραχμές. hílies **thra**hmés | *1 000 drachmas*
Είναι πολύ ακριβό. íne polí akrivó | *It is very expensive!*
Μπορείτε να πληρώσετε στο Ταμείο | *You can pay at the*
  boríte na plirósete sto tamío | *cash desk*

Numbers → 7, Clothes → 19

9   Money and Shopping

1 You want to change some money. What sign do you look for?

2 You enter a shop. The shop assistant asks you what you want. What does she say?

3 You are just looking. What do you tell the shop assistant?

4 You see a pretty vase. How do you ask how much it costs?

5 The shop assistant tells you it costs 1 000 drachmas. What does she say?

6 You think the vase is too expensive. What do you say?

7 The assistant asks you if you'd like anything else: What does she say?

8 You want to answer *No, thank you*. What do you say?

9 What is a special offer in Greek?

10 When the shop is closed what does the sign on the door
    say?

11 You pay the cashier. What is
    the sign for cashier in Greek?

Look at the receipt:

12 How many drachmas did the
    customer pay?

13 Say how much each of the
    goods cost.

- **Banks** are open daily from 8 am to 2 pm except Saturdays,
  Sundays and official public holidays. A few branches remain
  open in the afternoon and on Saturdays, for changing
  money only, but usually only in the larger towns.

- **Shops** are usually open from 8.30 am to 1.30 pm and from
  4.30 to 7.30 pm. In summer, they often remain open for
  longer hours. On Saturday most shops close for the day at
  3 pm and it is not customary to open on Sundays.

- Here are the names of some common shops:

σουπερμάρκετ	*supermarket*
παντοπωλείο (formal) ⎫ μπακάλικο (colloquial) ⎭	*grocer's*
γαλακτοπωλείο	*dairy*
αρτοπωλείο	*baker's*
κρεοπωλείο	*butcher's*
ζαχαροπλαστείο	*confectioner's*
φαρμακείο	*chemist's*
πρατήριο εφημερίδων	*news-stand*
περίπτερο	*kiosk*

a. Meals   **b.** Tableware   **c.** Breakfast   **d.** Snacks

a. ΦΑΓΗΤΟ φαγητό   fayitó — *food/meal*
ΠΡΩΙΝΟ πρωινό   proinó — *breakfast*
ΓΕΥΜΑ γεύμα   yévma — *lunch*
ΑΠΟΓΕΥΜΑΤΙΝΟ απογευματινό   apoyevmatinó — *afternoon snack*
ΔΕΙΠΝΟ δείπνο   thípno — *dinner*

Τι θα φάτε; ti tha fáte	*What will you eat?*
Τι θα πιείτε; ti tha pyíte	*What will you drink?*

b. φλιτζάνι flijáni — *cup*
ποτήρι potíri — *glass*
μπουκάλι bookáli — *bottle*
πιάτο pyáto — *plate/dish*
κουτάλι kootáli — *spoon*
πηρούνι piroóni — *fork*
μαχαίρι mahéri — *knife*
μεταλλικό νερό metalikó neró — *mineral water*

ένα ποτήρι νερό éna potíri neró	*a glass of water*
ένα μπουκάλι κρασί éna bookáli krasí	*a bottle of wine*
Άσπρο η κόκκινο κρασί; áspro i kókino krasí	*White or red wine?*

c. ψωμί psomí — *bread*
ψωμάκι psomáki — *roll*
μπισκότα biskóta — *biscuits*
βούτυρο voótiro — *butter*
μαρμελάδα marmelátha — *marmalade*
καφέ(ς) kafé(s) — *coffee*
τσάι tsái — *tea*

Θέλετε καφέ η τσάϊ; thélete kafé i tsái	*Would you like coffee or tea?*
Τσάι με γάλα, παρακαλώ tsái me ghála, parakaló	*tea with milk, please*
Παγωμένο καφέ paghoméno kafé	*iced coffee*
σκέτο καφέ skéto kafé	*black coffee*
Χυμό φρούτου himó froótoo	*fruit juice*

d. μεζέδες mezéthes — *snacks*
μεζές mezés — *snack*
ΤΟΣΤ τοστ tost — *toast*
ΣΑΝΤΟΥΙΤΣ σάντουϊτς sándooits — *sandwich*
ΣΟΥΒΛΑΚΙ σουβλάκι soovláki — *souvlaki (shish kebab)*
ΤΥΡΟΠΙΤΑ τυρόπιτα tirópita — *cheese pastry (pie)*
ΤΥΡΙ τυρί tirí — *cheese*
φέτα féta — *feta cheese*
ΓΙΑΟΥΡΤΙ γιαούρτι yaoórti — *yoghurt*
ταραμοσαλάτα taramosaláta — *taramasalata (fish roe paté)*
ΝΤΟΛΜΑΔΕΣ ντολμάδες dolmáthes — *dolmades (rice-filled vine leaves)*
λουκάνικα lookánika — *hot dogs*

έχετε σάντουϊτς; éhete sándooits	*Do you have any sandwiches?*
ένα σάντουϊτς με ζαμπόν éna sándooits me zabón.	*a ham sandwich*
ενα σάντουϊτς με τυρί éna sándooits me tirí	*a cheese sandwich*

Paying → 9, Restaurants → 11, Drinking → 14

10 Meals

1 What are the three meals of the day called in Greek?

2 What do you call these in Greek?

(a) (b) (c) (d) (e) (f) (g)

What are these typical Greek snacks called?

3   4

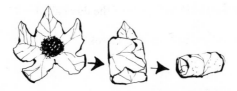

6 What's in this cup?

- **Meals:** Breakfast is usually very light in Greece, consisting simply of a cup of coffee and perhaps some biscuits or a roll with butter and marmalade. The **main meal** is traditionally lunch, eaten after 1 pm. Most offices, shops and banks close for a few hours in the afternoon, usually 1.30–4.30 pm, so that employees can go home, have lunch and a rest before going back to work. Dinner is eaten quite late from 9 pm onwards.

- **Food** is quite different from the rest of Europe and is very much inspired by the oriental style of eating both in the kind of dishes served and in eating habits.

- **Hors d'œuvres (μεζέδεϚ)** are eaten between meals, e.g. in the afternoon with a glass of ouzo. Some of the most popular ones are: olives, feta cheese, taramasalata, octopus, etc.

  Note: **Restaurants** are divided into classes and their prices are subject to Market Police Control, but they are often very reasonable when compared with English prices.

- **Night life** is lively in Greece and a visitor going out in the evening has a choice of places where the traditional **bouzouki** music is played.

11 Restaurants

a. Restaurants **b.** Service, Menu
c. Seasonings **d.** The Bill

a. ΕΣΤΙΑΤΟΡΙΟ	estiatório	*restaurant*
ΚΑΦΕΝΕΙΟ	kafenío	*café*
ΖΑΧΑΡΟΠΛΑΣΤΕΙΟ zaharoplastío		*pastry shop*
ΜΠΑΡ	bar	*bar*
ΤΑΒΕΡΝΑ	tavérna	*taverna (restaurant)*
ΨΑΡΟΤΑΒΕΡΝΑ	psarotavérna	*taverna specialising in seafood*
ΨΗΣΤΑΡΙΑ	psistaryá	*taverna specialising in charcoal-grilled food*
τραπέζι	trapézi	*table*
καρέκλα	karékla	*chair*

Ένα τραπέζι για δύο άτομα éna trapézi ya thío átoma	*A table for two people.*
Είναι αυτή η καρέκλα ελεύθερη; íne aftí i karékla eléftheri	*Is this seat free?*
Ναι, βέβαια! Ne, vévea	*Yes, of course!*

b. κατάλογος katáloghos — *menu*
ΜΕΝΟΥ μενού menoó — *complete, fixed price meal*
πιάτο pyáto — *course, dish*

Θέλω κάτι να φάω.	*I'd like something*
thélo káti na fáo	*to eat.*
Τον κατάλογο, παρακαλώ.	*The menu, please.*
ton katálogho parakaló	
Τι θέλετε να φάτε;	*What would you like*
ti thélete na fáte	*to eat?*
Τί θέλετε να πιείτε;	*What would you like*
ti thélete na pyíte	*to drink?*

c. **ΖΑΧΑΡΗ** ζάχαρη záhari — *sugar*
ΑΛΑΤΙ αλάτι aláti — *salt*
ΠΙΠΕΡΙ πιπέρι pipéri — *pepper*
ΛΑΔΙ λάδι láthi — *oil*

Μου δίνετε το αλάτι, παρακαλώ;	*Would you give me the*
moo thínete to aláti parakaló	*salt, please?*
Μάλιστα, ορίστε! málista, oríste	*Yes, certainly, here*
	you are!

d. γκαρσόν garsón — *waiter*
ΛΟΓΑΡΙΑΣΜΟ(Σ) λογαριασμό(ς) — *bill*
logharyasmó(s)
ΑΠΟΔΕΙΞΗ απόδειξη apóthiksi — *receipt*

Τον λογαριασμό, παρακαλώ	*The bill, please.*
ton logharyasmó parakaló	
Θέλω να πληρώσω	*I'd like to pay*
thélo na pliróso	
Περιλαμβάνεται το φιλοδώρημα;	*Is service included?*
perilamvánete to filothórima	
Εντάξει! endáksi	*It's all right.*
	(Keep the change).
Το φαγητό ήταν πολύ καλό.	*The meal was*
to faghitó ítan polí kaló	*very good.*

Toilets → 6, Tableware → 10, Paying → 9, Drinks → 14

11 Restaurants

1 Where do you go:
   (a) to have coffee and a cake?
   (b) to have lunch or dinner?
   (c) to have a drink?

2 You want to ask if a seat is
   free. What do you say?

3 Tell the waiter you'd
   like something to eat.

4 Tell the waiter you'd
   like the menu.

5 You would like to have the
   salt. What do you say?

6 After you've ordered your food, the waiter asks what
   you'd like to drink. What does he say?

7 After the meal you'd like to pay. What do you say to the
   waiter?

8 You want to ask if service is included. What do you say?

9 The waiter wants to give you back the change, but you
   want him to keep it as a tip. What do you say?

What is in these containers?

10   11

- **Greek cooking** offers a wide variety of dishes which can be found in most restaurants and **tavernas**. It is quite normal in a local taverna to go to the kitchen and choose what you want. The tavernas situated along the coast usually specialise in seafood. Fish is often ordered by the kilo (2.2 lb).

- In the Athens area most typical **tavernas** are found in **Plaka**, the old part of the city at the foot of the Acropolis. Those specialising in seafood are mostly found along the **Akti Apollonos** seashore.

- Although the bill usually includes the service charge, it is customary to leave an additional **tip** of approximately 10% for the waiter.

12 Starters, Meat, Fish

a. Starters, Soups **b.** Meat **c.** Poultry, Eggs **d.** Fish

a. ΜΕΖΕΔΕΣ μεζέδες mezéthes — *starters* (colloquial)
ΟΡΕΚΤΙΚΑ ορεκτικά orektiká — *starters* (formal)
ΣΟΥΠΑ σούπα soópa — *soup*

ΣΟΥΠΑ ΗΜΕΡΑΣ σούπα ημέρας soópa iméras	*soup of the day*
ΝΤΟΜΑΤΟΣΟΥΠΑ ντοματόσουπα domatósoopa	*tomato soup*
ΚΟΤΟΣΟΥΠΑ κοτόσουπα kotósoopa	*chicken soup*
σούπα αυγολέμονο soópa avgholémono	*egg and lemon soup with rice*
ψαρόσουπα psarósoopa	*fish soup*

b. κρέας kréas — *meat*
ΑΡΝΙ αρνί arní — *mutton*
ΑΡΝΑΚΙ αρνάκι arnáki — *lamb*
ΚΑΤΣΙΚΑΚΙ κατσικάκι katsikáki — *kid*
ΜΟΣΧΑΡΙ μοσχάρι moshári — *beef*

ΜΟΣΧΑΡΑΚΙ μοσχαράκι	mosharáki	*veal*
ΜΠΙΦΤΕΚΙ μπιφτέκι	biftéki	*steak*
ΧΟΙΡΙΝΟ χοιρινό	hirinó	*pork*
ΦΙΛΕΤΟ φιλέτο	filéto	*fillet steak*
μπριζόλες	brizóles	*chops*
παϊδάκια	paithákya	*cutlets*
ΚΕΦΤΕΔΕΣ κεφτέδες	keftéthes	*meat balls*
ΜΟΥΣΑΚΑ(Σ) μουσακά(ς)	moosaka(s)	*moussaka*
ΠΑΣΤΙΤΣΙΟ παστίτσιο	pastítsio	*macaroni with minced meat in filo pastry*
σάλτσα	sáltsa	*sauce*

Τι σερβίρετε με το κρέας/ψάρι; ti servírete me to kréas/psári	*What do you serve with the meat/fish?*
Πως θέλετε το μπιφτέκι σας; pos thélete to biftéki sas	*How do you like your steak done?*
λίγο ψημένο lígho psiméno	*rare*
μέτριο métrio	*medium*
καλοψημένο kalopsiméno	*well-done*

c.

κότα	kóta	*chicken*
κοτόπουλο	kotópoolo	*young chicken*
αυγό	avghó	*egg*
ΟΜΕΛΕΤΤΑ ομελέττα	omeléta	*omelette*

d.

ΨΑΡΙ ψάρι	psári	*fish*
χταπόδι	htapóthi	*octopus*
καλαμαράκια	kalamarákya	*squid*
μπαρμπούνι	barboóni	*red mullet*
τσιπούρα	tsipoóra	*snapper*
μπακαλιάρος	bakaliáros	*cod*
τόνος	tónos	*tuna*
γαρίδες	gharíthes	*shrimps*
καραβίδες	karavíthes	*crayfish*
αστακός	astakós	*lobster*
ταραμάς	taramás	*fish roe*

ψάρι πλακί psári plakí	*stewed fish*
ψάρι στο φούρνο psári sto foórno	*baked fish*
ψάρι τηγανητό psári tighanitó	*fried fish*
ψάρι στη σχάρα psári sti shára	*grilled fish*
ψάρι στα κάρβουνα psári sta kárvoona	*fish baked on charcoal*

Ask the waiter for the following:

1 Soup of the day.

2 Fillet steak.

3 Lamb.

4 Omelette.

5 Fish.

6 Fried fish.

7 Grilled fish.

What are the following called in Greek?

8

9

 mashed potato/cheese
 sliced aubergine
 minced meat
 sliced potato

10   11

- Greek people spend a considerable amount of time eating **hors d'oeuvres** (ορεκτικά or μεζέδες) before they proceed with the main dish.

- Some of the most typical Greek μεζέδες are:

  ταραμοσαλάτα: a paté of smoked cod's roe blended with bread, olive-oil and lemon.

  μελιτζανοσαλάτα: aubergine baked on charcoal, mashed and mixed with olive oil and lemon.

  τζατζίκι: a paté of yogurt, cucumber and garlic.

  καλαμαράκια: young squid (usually crisply fried)

  χταπόδι: octopus (grilled on charcoal, or fried)

- Some of the most typical **main dishes** are:

  αρνάκι σούβλας: lamb roast on a spit.

  κοκορέτσι: spiced pieces of heart, liver and kidney, lashed with strips of entrail to a skewer and grilled.

  μουσακά(ς): layers of sliced aubergine and minced meat covered with cheese sauce, baked in the oven.

  γιουβέτσι: meat with spaghetti and tomatoes baked in the oven.

  στιφάδο: a stew of rabbit or hare cooked in oil, wine, herbs, small onions.

  ψάρι στη σχάρα: grilled fish.

- The main course is usually served with **χωριάτικη σαλάτα** – salad made with tomatoes, green pepper, cucumber, féta cheese, onions and olives.

- The most popular cheese in Greece is féta **φέτα**. It can be soft, hard or crumbly and very salty. It is often eaten in salads or in the popular **τυρόπιτες**.

13   Vegetables, Fruit, Desserts

a. Vegetables   b. Fruit   c. Desserts, Sweets

a.

ΛΑΧΑΝΙΚΑ λαχανικά	lahaniká	*vegetables*
ΠΑΤΑΤΕΣ πατάτες	patátes	*potatoes*
πατάτες τηγανητές patátes tighanités		*potato chips*
μπιζέλια	bizélya	*peas*
καρότα	karóta	*carrots*
σπανάκι	spanáki	*spinach*
μελιτζάνες	melijánes	*aubergines*
αγκινάρες	anginares	*artichokes*
πιπεριές	piperyés	*peppers*
κρεμμύδια	kremíthya	*onions*
(ν)τομάτες	domátes	*tomato*
ελιές	elyés	*olives*
κολοκυθάκια	kolokithákya	*courgettes*
χόρτα	hórta	*greens*
ραδίκια	rathíkya	*greens (wild)*
μπάμιες	bámyes	*ladies' fingers (okra)*
μαρούλι	maroóli	*lettuce*
λάχανο	láhano	*cabbage*
κουνουπίδι	koonoopíthi	*cauliflower*
αγγούρι	angoóri	*cucumber*
ΤΖΑΤΖΙΚΙ τζατζίκι	jajíki	*yoghurt with garlic and cucumber*
σκόρδο	skórtho	*garlic*
σκορδαλιά	skorthalyá	*garlic sauce*
ρύζι	rízi	*rice*
ρεβύθια	revíthya	*chick-peas*
φακές	fakés	*lentils*
φασόλια	fasólya	*beans*

ντοματοσαλάτα domatosaláta	*tomato salad*
χωριάτικη σαλάτα horiátiki saláta	*salad with tomatoes, green pepper, feta cheese, onions and olives*
ντομάτες γεμιστές domátes yemistés	*stuffed tomatoes*
μελιτζάνες γεμιστές melijánes yemistés	*stuffed aubergines*
μπάμιες γιαχνί bámyes yahní	*okra braised in oil with tomatoes and onions*

b. ΦΡΟΥΤΑ φρούτα froóta

μήλα míla	*apples*
πορτοκάλι portokáli	*orange*
λεμόνι lemóni	*lemon*
πεπόνι pepóni	*melon*
καρπούζι karpoózi	*water melon*
σταφύλια stafílya	*grapes*
σύκα síka	*figs*
κεράσια kerásya	*cherries*
βερύκοκα veríkoka	*apricots*
ροδάκινα rothákina	*peaches*
αχλάδια ahláthya	*pears*
φράουλες fráooles	*strawberries*
καρύδια karíthya	*walnuts*
αμύγδαλα amígthala	*almonds*
φυστίκια fistíkya	*pistachio nuts*
πασατέμπος pasatémpos	*pumpkin seeds*

Ένα καρπούζι, παρακαλώ éna karpoózi parakaló	*One water-melon, please.*
Δύο λεμόνια, παρακαλώ thío lemónya parakaló	*Two lemons, please.*
ΦΡΟΥΤΟΣΑΛΑΤΑ frootosaláta	*fruit salad*

c. ΓΛΥΚΑ γλυκά ghliká

ΠΑΣΤΕΣ πάστες pástes	*tarts*
πάστα αμυγδάλου pásta amigtháloo	*almond tart*
ΠΑΓΩΤΟ παγωτό paghotó	*ice cream*
κέϊκ kéik	*cake*
μπακλαβά(ς) baklavá(s)	*baklava (flaky pastry filled with nuts and honey)*
λουκουμάδες lookoomáthes	*doughnuts dipped in honey*
μηλόπιτα milópita	*apple pie*
ρυζόγαλο rizóghalo	*rice pudding*

desserts, sweets

Ένα παγωτό, παρακαλώ éna paghotó parakaló	*An ice cream please*
παγωτό φράουλα paghotó fráoola	*strawberry ice cream*
βανίλια vanilya	*vanilla*
σοκολάτα sokoláta	*chocolate*

13 Vegetables, Fruit, Desserts

What are the following in Greek? Say you like them, or you
don't like it/them.

Start: marési **μ' αρέσει**... (sing.)

marésoon **μ' αρέσουν**... (plural)

Examples: μ' αρέσει το καρπούζι (*I like [the] water melon*)

μ' αρέσουν τα σταφύλια (*I like [the] grapes*)

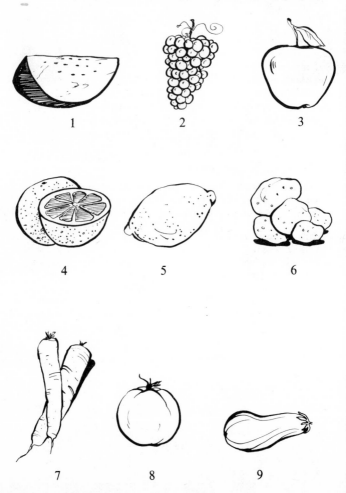

10 You are looking for 'Desserts' on the menu. What are they called in Greek?

11 Say you want:
   (*a*) a pastry filled with nuts and honey.
   (*b*) an ice cream.
   (*c*) an orange.

- In Greece there are nuts and seeds everywhere to eat as a **snack**, which you can buy from street vendors. The most common are pistachios (which are usually not coloured green in Greece), almonds, sunflower seeds, etc.

- **Rice** is one of the staple foods in Greece. It was brought from Asia by Alexander the Great. Pilaf (πιλάφι) is rice which is cooked with herbs.

- The vocabulary in units 12 and 13 is sufficient to help you get along with any Greek menu. In places where there are a lot of tourists dining, the menus are usually printed in two languages: Greek and English.

14 Drinking and Smoking

a. Non-alcoholic Drinks **b.** Alcoholic Drinks
c. Smoking

a. ΠΟΤΑ ποτά potá — *drinks/beverages*
ΑΝΑΨΥΚΤΙΚΑ αναψυκτικά anapsiktiká — *refreshments*
χυμός φρούτου himós froótoo — *(fresh) fruit juice*
πορτοκαλάδα portokalátha — *orangeade*
λεμονάδα lemonátha — *lemonade*
ΝΕΡΟ νερό neró — *water*
μεταλλικό νερό metalikó neró — *mineral water*
ΚΑΦΕ(Σ) καφέ(ς) kafé(s) — *coffee*
παγωμένο(ς) καφέ(ς) paghoméno(s) kafé(s) — *iced coffee*
εσπρέσσο espréso — *espresso*
καπουτσίνο kapootsíno — *cappuccino*
φραπέ frapé — *coffee with ice cream*
τσάϊ tsáï — *tea*
γάλα ghála — *milk*

μίλκ σέϊκ	"milk shake"	*milk shake*
σοκολάτα	sokoláta	*chocolate*

Θέλω...	thélo	*I want.../I would like*
Ένα ποτήρι νερό	ένα potíri neró	*A glass of water*
Μία κόκα-κόλα	mia kóka-kóla	*A Coke*
Δύο καφέδες Νές.	thío kaféthes nés	*Two Nescafés*
με/χωρίς γαλα	me/horís ghála	*With/without milk*
με/χωρίζ ξάχαρη	me/horís záhari	*With/without sugar*

b.

ΜΠΥΡΑ μπύρα	bíra	*beer*
ΟΙΝΟΣ οίνος	ínos	*wine (formal Greek)*
ΚΡΑΣΙ κρασί	krasí	*wine (colloquial)*
ΡΕΤΣΙΝΑ ρετσίνα	retsína	*retsina (resinated wine)*
ΟΥΖΟ ούζο	oózo	*anisette*
λικέρ	likér	*liqueur*
κονιάκ	konyiák	*cognac*
τιρμπουσόν	tirboosón	*corkscrew*

ΛΕΥΚΟ ΚΡΑΣΙ λευκό κρασί		*white wine*
lefkó krasí		
ΚΟΚΚΙΝΟ ΚΡΑΣΙ κόκκινο κρασί		*red wine*
kókino krasí		
ΚΡΑΣΙ ΓΛΥΚΟ κρασί γλυκό		*sweet wine*
krasí ghlikó		
ΚΡΑΣΙ ΞΗΡΟ κρασί ξηρό		*dry wine*
krasí ksiró		
Ένα ποτήρι κρασί	ένα potíri krasí	*a glass of wine*
Ένα μπουκάλι κρασί.		*a bottle of wine*
ένα bookáli krasi		
Μία μπύρα, παρακαλώ.		*A beer, please.*
mía bíra parakaló		
Στην υγειά σας!	stin iyá sas	*Cheers!*

c.

τσιγάρο	tsigháro	*cigarette*
αναπτήρα(ς)	anaptíra(s)	*lighter*
σπίρτα	spírta	*matches*
τασάκι	tasáki	*ashtray*

Ένα πακέτο τσιγάρα.		*A packet of cigarettes.*
ένα pakéto tsighára		
ΜΗ ΚΑΠΝΙΖΕΤΕ	mi kapnízete	*No smoking!*
ΑΠΑΓΟΡΕΥΕΤΑΙ ΤΟ ΚΑΠΝΙΣΜΑ		*No smoking!*
apaghorévete to kápnisma		

14 Drinking and Smoking

Order the following drinks from the waiter:

1 an orangeade.

2 a lemonade.

3 a Coke.

4 two Nescafés.

5 a tea with milk.

6 a beer.

7 a bottle of red wine.

8 a glass of water.

9 an ouzo.

How do you say the following in Greek?

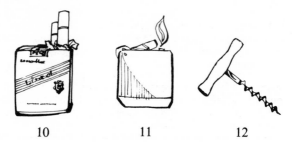

10   11   12

- Greek mineral water **νερό,** e.g. ´Ηβη (pronounced: ívi) is one of the most popular.

- Authentic Greek **coffee** καφέ(ς) is served in small cups, never with milk or cream. You can drink it:
without sugar	σκέτο(ς)	skéto(s)
slightly sweetened:	μέτριο(ς)	métrio(s)
very sweet	γλυκό(ς)	ghlikó(s)
A glass of water is always served together with the coffee to wash it down.

- In Greece, **Retsina wine** is very popular. It has a taste of resin and is usually better from the barrel than bottled. Retsina tastes best when chilled; it can also be drunk mixed with water.

- **Ouzo** is a famous clear spirit distilled from grapes and flavoured with aniseed. It has a high alcoholic content. When mixed with water, ouzo turns milky white. Greeks eat hors d'oeuvres μεζέδες with ouzo.

15 Sightseeing and Entertainment

a. Tourism **b.** Sightseeing **c.** Entertainment
d. Admission

a. τουρίστας toorístas   *tourist (m.)*
   ταξίδι taksíthi   *trip*
   προσπέκτους prospéktoos   *brochure*
   Τουριστική Αστυνομία   *Tourist Police*
      tooristikí astinomía
   αρχαιολογικός τόπος   *archaeological site*
      arheoloyikós tópos

Που είναι το Γραφείο Τουρισμού;	*Where is the Tourist*
poo íne to grafío toorismoó	*Office?*
Θέλω ένα τουριστικό οδηγό	*I would like a guide-*
thélo éna tooristikó othighó	*book.*
στα αγγλικά sta angliká	*in English.*

b. ΜΟΥΣΕΙΟ μουσείο moosío   *museum*
   μνημείο mnimío   *monument*
   αρχαιότητες arheótites   *antiquities*
   ναός naós   *temple*
   κολώνα kolóna   *column*
   αμφορέας amforéas   *amphora*
   αμφιθέατρο amfithéatro   *amphitheatre*
   έκθεση ékthesi   *exhibition*
   πινακοθήκη pinakothíki   *art gallery*
   άγαλμα ághalma   *statue*
   στάδιο státhio   *stadium*
   κατακόμβες katakómves   *catacombs*
   εκκλησία eklisía   *church*
   μοναστήρι monastíri   *monastery*
   εικόνα ikóna   *icon*
   άγιος, αγία áyios, ayía   *saint (male/female)*

Η πύλη των λεόντων στις Μυκήνες	*The Lion's Gate at*
i pili ton leóndon stis Mikínes	*Mycenae*
Είσοδος σταδίου της Ολυμπίας.	*Entrance to the stadium*
ísothos stathíoo tis Olimbías.	*at Olympia.*
Ο Δίας. o thías	*Zeus.*

c. μπουζούκι boozoóki — *bouzouki*
κιθάρα kithára — *guitar*
φλάουτο fláooto — *flute*
ντισκοτέκ "discothéque" — *discothéque*
νυχτερινό κέντρο nihterinó kéndro — *night club*
φεστιβάλ κρασιού festivál krasyoó — *wine festival*
λαϊκός χορός laikós horós — *folk dancing*
σινεμά sinemá — *cinema*
φίλμ film — *film*
θέατρο théatro — *theatre*
αρχαία ελληνική τραγωδία
  arhéa eliniki traghothía — *classical Greek tragedy*
κωμωδία komothía — *comedy*
δράμα thráma — *drama*
πρόγραμμα próghrama — *programme*

Τι παίζει; ti pézi	*What is on?*
Τι ώρα αρχίζει; ti óra arhízi	*What time does it start?*
Τι ώρα τελειώνει; ti óra telióni	*What time does it end?*

d. ΩΡΕΣ ΛΕΙΤΟΥΡΓΙΑΣ — *opening hours*
  ώρες λειτουργίας óres litooryias
ΑΝΟΙΚΤΟ ανοικτό aniktó — *open*
ΚΛΕΙΣΤΟ κλειστό klistó — *closed*
ΕΙΣΟΔΟΣ είσοδος ísothos — *entrance*
ΕΞΟΔΟΣ έξοδος éksothos — *exit*
ΕΙΣΙΤΗΡΙΟ εισιτήριο isitírio — *ticket*
ΞΕΝΑΓΟΣ ξεναγός ksenaghós — *(tourist) guide*

Πότε είναι το μουσείο ανοικτό; póte íne to moosío aniktó	*When is the museum open?*
Πόσο κοστίζει η είσοδος; póso kostízi i ísothos	*How much is the admission charge?*
Έχει έκπτωση για φοιτητές/παιδιά; éhi ékptosi ya fitités/pethyá	*Is there a reduction for students/children?*
ΕΙΣΟΔΟΣ ΕΛΕΥΘΕΡΑ ísothos elefthéra	*admission free*
ΜΗΝ ΑΓΓΙΖΕΤΕ min angízete	*do not touch*
ΑΠΑΓΟΡΕΥΟΝΤΑΙ ΟΙ ΦΩΤΟΓΡΑΦΙΕΣ apaghorévonde i fotoghrafíes	*photographs are prohibited*

15 Sightseeing and Entertainment

Do you recognise these relics? Can you name them?

1   Lion's Gate at Mycenae

2   Zeus

3   'Hermes', by Praxiteles

4   Entrance to the stadium at Olympia

5 How do you ask for an entrance ticket to a museum?

6 You want to ask how much is the admission. What do you say?

- The most important **museums** in Athens are:
National Archaeological Museum ΕΘΝΙΚΟ ΑΡΧΑΙΟΛΟ-ΓΙΚΟ ΜΟΥΣΕΙΟ. The Museum displays finds from all parts of the ancient Greek world which date from Neolithic times to the last years of the Roman Empire (open daily 08.00–17.00, Mondays 11.00–15.00, Sundays 09.00–16.00).

The archaeological site of Acropolis ΑΚΡΟΠΟΛΙΣ (open daily 07.30–19.30).

Acropolis Museum ΜΟΥΣΕΙΟΝ ΑΚΡΟΠΟΛΕΩΣ.
The Museum contains mainly pedimental sculpture, reliefs and statues found on the rock of Acropolis, which formed part of the decoration of its buildings or were dedicated to the goddess Athena (open daily 09.00–15.00 except Tuesdays).

Ancient Agora ΑΡΧΑΙΑ ΑΓΟΡΑ (open daily 09.00–15.15 except Tuesdays).

Byzantine Museum ΒΥΖΑΝΤΙΝΟ ΜΟΥΣΕΙΟ.
The exhibits cover the early Christian, the Byzantine and the post-Byzantine periods (open daily 08.00–18.00, Sundays 10.00–14.00, closed on Mondays).

- In the summer, **ancient drama** is presented at the open theatre of Herodus Atticus (near the Acropolis) or at Epidauros (in the Peloponnese) by the National Greek Theatre Company.

- From May to September, there are performances of Greek **folk dancing** at the open-air theatre on Filopappus Hill in Athens.

- Every summer, from early July to early September, a **Wine Festival** takes place at **Dafni** (11 km from Athens). A large variety of Greek wines awaits the visitor and can be tasted at no charge. A self-service taverna is also in operation, offering typical Greek specialities. There are dance floors, singing and various contests, open to participation by any visitor. A regular bus service runs from Athens to Dafni.

16   Excursions and Recreation

a. Excursions   **b.** Scenery   **c.** Sports, Activities
d. Photography

a. εκδρομή ekthromí	*excursion*
γύρος yíros	*tour* (colloquial)
περιοδεία periothía	*tour* (formal)

Τουριστική εκδρομή tooristikí ekthromí	*Tourist excursion*
Πόσο κοστίζει η εκδρομή; póso kostízi i ekthromí	*How much does the excursion cost?*
Τι ώρα θα ξεκινήσουμε/γυρίσουμε; ti óra tha ksekinísoome/yirísoome	*What time shall we leave/return?*
Υπάρχει ξεναγός που να μιλάει αγγλικά; ipárhi ksenaghós poo na milái angliká	*Is there a guide who speaks English?*

b. θάλασσα thálasa	*sea*
ακτή aktí	*coast*
κόλπος kólpos	*gulf*
δελφίνι thelfíni	*dolphin*
καρχαρίας karharías	*shark*
νησί nisí	*island*
ισθμός isthmós	*isthmus*
ποτάμι potámi	*river*
βουνό voonó	*mountain*

Μεσόγειος θάλασσα mesóyios thálasa	*Mediterranean Sea*
Νησί Μύκονος nisí míkonos	*(Island of) Mykonos*
Ισθμός της Κορίνθου isthmós tis korínthoo	*Isthmus of Corinth*

c. ΠΛΑΖ πλαζ plaz	*beach*
πισίνα pisína	*swimming-pool*
παραλία paralía	*shore*
άμμο(ς) ámos	*sand*
ομπρέλλα ηλίου ombréla ilíoo	*(beach) umbrella*
πολυθρόνα polithróna	*deck-chair*
στρώμα φουσκωτό stróma fooskotó	*air mattress*

κολυμπώ kolimbó	*I swim*
ακτοφύλακας aktofílakas	*lifeguard*
κανώ kanó	*canoe*
βάρκα várka	*rowing-boat*
βάρκα με μηχανή várka me mihaní	*motor-boat*
βάρκα με πανί várka me paní	*sailing-boat*
ΤΕΝΝΙΣ τέννις "ténnis"	*tennis*

Είναι καθαρή η θάλασσα; ine katharí i thálasa	*Is the sea clean?*
Είναι βαθειά εδώ; ine vathyá **ethó**	*Is it deep here?*
Πηγαίνω για κολύμπι. piyéno ya kolímbi	*I am going for a swim.*
υποβρύχιο ψάρεμα. ipovríhio psárema	*under-water fishing*
θαλάσσιο σκι thalásio ski	*water-skiing*
σέρφ "surf"	*surfing*
Έχει καμπίνες με ντους; éhi cambínes me doos	*Are there any cabins with showers?*
Θέλω να νοικιάσιω . . . thélo na nikyáso	*I would like to hire . . .*
Θέλω ν' αγοράσω . . . thélo naghoráso	*I would like to buy . . .*
ΑΠΑΓΟΡΕΥΕΤΑΙ ΤΟ ΚΟΛΥΜΠΙ apaghorévete to kolímbi	*Swimming is forbidden.*

d. φωτογραφική μηχανή fotoghrafikí mihaní	*camera*
φωτογραφία fotoghrafía	*photograph*
ΦΙΛΜ φιλμ film	*film*
φλας flas	*flash*
μπαταρία bataría	*battery*
σλάιτς "slides"	*slides*

Επιτρέπεται να φωτογραφίσω; epitrépete na fotoghrafíso	*Is one allowed to take pictures?*
Ένα φίλμ για τη μηχανή μου éna film ya ti mihaní moo	*A film for my camera.*
Ένα έγχρωμο φίλμ. éna énhromo film	*A colour film.*

16 Excursions and Recreation

What do you see in these pictures? Answer in Greek, starting with βλέπω . . . vlépo (I see . . .)

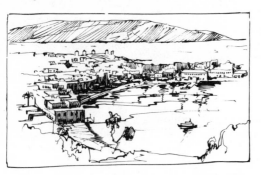

1 Mykonos

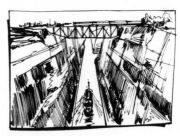

2 Isthmus of Corinth

3 Dolphins

4 What sign do you look for if you want to go to: (*a*) the beach? (*b*) the swimming-pool?

What are the following in Greek?

5 6 7

You would like to buy the following items. Ask for them in Greek, beginning with **θέλω ν' αγοράσω** ... (*I would like to buy* ...)

8 9 10

11 Say you would like to hire (*a*) a canoe; (*b*) a rowing-boat.

- There are numerous travel agencies in Athens which organise sightseeing tours within the city, or conducted excursions by motorcoach to popular tourist areas and archaeological sites outside the capital.

- Most public **beaches** in Greece offer facilities such as changing rooms (**καμπίνες**), showers, sun umbrellas, deck-chairs, piers, canoes, areas for various games (tennis-courts, etc.), children's playgrounds, snack-bars, restaurants, self-service shops, discotheques.

- You are usually allowed to photograph everything in Greece, except for important military and strategic installations, e.g. airfields.

- **Photographing** with a simple camera without tripod is permitted at archaeological sites, but inside museums it is allowed only after payment of an additional admission fee. For a tripod-mounted camera, a permit must be obtained from the Antiquities Authority in each district.

17 The Weather

a. The weather   **b.** Good weather
c. Bad weather   **d.** Cold weather

a.

ΚΑΙΡΟΣ καιρός	kerós	*weather*
προβλέπεται	provlépete	*it is forecast*
θερμοκρασία	thermokrasía	*temperature*

Πως είναι ο καιρός σήμερα; pos ine o kerós símera	*What's the weather like today?*
Τι καιρός προβλέπεται για αύριο; ti kerós provlépete ya ávrio	*What is the weather forecast for tomorrow?*
Ο καιρός . . . ο kerós	*The weather . . .*
. . . στην Αττικη. stin attikí	*. . . in Attica.*
. . . στη Θεσσαλονίκη. sti thessaloníki	*. . . in Thessalonica.*

b.

καλός καιρός	kalós kerós	*good weather*
ήλιος	ílyos	*sun*
λιακάδα	lyakátha	*sunshine*
αίθριος	éthrios	*fair*
ζέστη	zésti	*warm, hot*

Ο ουρανός είναι καθαρός. o ooranós íne katharós	*The sky is clear.*
Ο καιρός είναι καλός. o kerós íne kalós	*The weather is good.*
Ο ήλιος λάμπει. o ílyos lámbi	*The sun is shining.*
Τι θαυμάσιος καιρός! Ti thavmásios kerós	*What lovely weather!*
Κάνει ζέστη. káni zésti	*It's hot.*
Το νερό είναι ζεστό to neró íne zestó	*The water is warm.*

c.

άσχημος καιρός áshimos kerós	*bad weather*
συννεφιά sinefyá	*cloudy*
αστάθεια astáthia	*changeable weather*
βροχή vrohí	*rain*
καταιγίδα kateyítha	*thunderstorm*
θύελλα thíela	*storm*
άνεμος ánemos	*wind (formal)*
αέρας aéras	*wind (colloquial)*
ήρεμη íremi	*calm*
ταραγμένη taraghméni	*rough sea*
κυματώδης kimatóthis	*very rough sea*

Βρέχει. vréhi	*It is raining.*
Είναι συννεφιά. íne sinefyá	*It is cloudy*
Θα βρέξει. tha vréksi	*It is going to rain.*
φυσάει αέρας. fisái aéras	*It is windy.*
Ο αέρας είναι πολύ δυνατός. o aéras íne polí thinatós	*The wind is very strong.*
Η θάλασσα είναι ήρεμη. i thálasa íne íremi	*The sea is calm.*
Ο καιρός θα καλυτερέψει. o kerós tha kaliterépsi	*The weather will improve.*

d.

κρύο krío	*cold*
δροσιά throsyá	*cool*
ομίχλη omíhli	*mist, fog*
χιόνι hyóni	*snow*
χαλάζι halázi	*hail*

κάνει κρύο. káni krío	*It is cold.*
έχει ομίχλη. éhi omíhli	*It is foggy.*

Time, Dates → 8

17 The Weather

Look at this weather map of Greece from the newspaper 'ΜΕΣΗΜΒΡΙΝΗ':

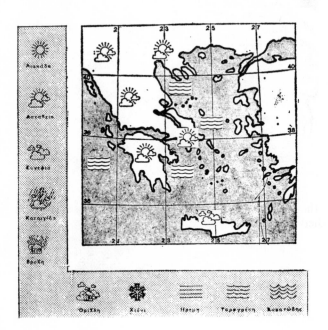

1 What is the weather like in northern Greece?

2 What is the weather like in Athens?

3 What is the weather like in Crete?

What's the weather like?

4   5

Read the following excerpts from these weather reports and
say whether the forecast is for good or bad weather.

	Καλός Καιρός	Άσχημος Καιρός
6 Ο καιρός είναι αίθριος . . .	○	○
7 Στην Αττική προβλέπε- ται συννεφιά με βροχή . . .	○	○
8 Η θάλασσα είναι κυματώδης . . .	○	○

- There are **weather reports** in all Greek newspapers, but no
  weather map. The headline is usually.
  ο καιρός σήμερα (*Today's Weather*).

- The Athens radio station broadcasts a short **news programme in English** every day at 7.30 am, together with the
  weather forecast.

18 Post Office and Telephone

a. Post Office **b.** Letters, Postcards
c. Telephone **d.** Telegrams

a. ΤΑΧΥΔΡΟΜΕΙΟ ταχυδρομείο _post office_
   tahi**th**romío

Που είναι το ταχυδρομείο;	_Where is the Post_
poo íne to tahi**th**romío	_Office?_
Τι ώρα ανοίγει; ti óra aníyi	_What time does it open?_
Τι ώρα κλείνει; ti óra klíni	_What time does it_
	close?

b. γράμμα ghráma — *letter*
κάρτα kárta — *postcard*
φάκελος fákelos — *envelope*
διεύθυνση thiéfthinsi — *address*
ΓΡΑΜΜΑΤΟΣΗΜΑ ghramatósima — *stamps*
γραμματόσημο ghramatósimo — *stamp*
ΔΕΜΑΤΑ δέματα thémata — *parcels*
στυλό stiló — *ballpoint pen*
γραμματοκιβώτιο ghramatokivótio — *letter-box*
αεροπορικώς aeroporikós — *airmail*

Πόσο κοστίζει μία κάρτα για την Αγγλία; póso kostízi mía kárta ya tin anglia	*How much is a postcard to England?*
Που είναι το γραμματοκιβώτιο; poo íne to ghramatokivótio	*Where is the letter-box?*
Μερικά γραμματόσημα, παρακαλώ. meriká ghramatósima parakaló	*Some stamps, please.*

c. ΤΗΛΕΦΩΝΟ τηλέφωνο (Τηλ.) — *telephone, telephone*
tiléfono — *number*
τηλεφωνικός κατάλογος — *telephone directory*
tilefonikós katáloghos
ακουστικό akoostikó — *receiver*

Έχετε τηλέφωνο; éhete tiléphono	*Is there a phone here?*
Μπορώ να τηλεφωνήσω; boró na tilefoníso	*May I use the phone?*
Μιλάτε αγγλικά; miláte angliká	*Do you speak English?*
Εμπρός; embrós	*Hello? (on answering phone)*
Μια στιγμή. mya stighmí	*One moment.*

d. τηλεγράφημα tileghráfima — *telegram*

Που είναι ο ΟΤΕ poo íne o oté	*Where is the OTE?*
Θέλω να στείλω ένα τηλεγράφημα στην Αγγλία. thélo na stílo éna tileghráfima stin anglía	*I want to send a telegram to England.*
Πόσο κοστίζει η λέξη; póso kostízi i léksi	*How much is it per word?*

What are these called in Greek?

7 You want to know the postage for a postcard to England. What do you ask for?

8 You want to buy some stamps. What do you say?

9 What is this called in Greek?

10 You want a telephone directory. What is it called in Greek?

- Note the two kinds of letter-boxes:
    for foreign mail: ΕΞΩΤΕΡΙΚΟΥ.
    for domestic mail: ΕΣΩΤΕΡΙΚΟΥ.

- The **post office** and the **telephone/telegraph** office are two separate facilities in Greece. *OTE* (Greek Telephone Corporation) is responsible for telephone and telegrams.

- International area codes:
    England, Northern Ireland   0044
    USA   001
    Canada   001

- To make a telephone call in Greece:
    1. Lift receiver and wait for tone. 2. Insert coins. 3. Dial number. 4. Now you can make a 6 minute call.

19 Clothing and Toiletries

a. Clothing **b.** Socks and Shoes **c.** Colours
d. Toiletries **e.** At the Hairdresser

a.

μπλούζα blóoza	*blouse*
φόρεμα fórema	*dress*
φούστα fóosta	*skirt*
πουλόβερ poolóver	*pullover/sweater*
ζακέτα zakéta	*jacket*
πουκάμισο pookámiso	*shirt*
πανταλόνι pantalóni	*trousers*
τζην(ς) dzin(s)	*jeans*
σορτ sort	*shorts*
ζώνη zóni	*belt*
καπέλο kapélo	*hat*
μαγιό mayó	*bathing suit/trunks*
μπικίνι bikíni	*bikini*
ΔΟΚΙΜΑΣΤΗΡΙΑ δοκιμαστήρια thokimastíria	*changing-rooms*

Θέλω μία μπλούζα thélo mía blóoza	*I'd like a blouse*
Θέλω ένα πουκάμισο thélo éna pookámiso	*I'd like a shirt*
Τι μέγεθος είναι αυτό; ti méyethos íne aftó	*What size is this?*
Μπορώ να το δοκιμάσω; boró na to thokimáso	*Can I try it on?*
είναι πολύ μεγάλο/μικρό/στενό/ κοντό/μακρύ íne polí meghálo/mikró/stenó/ kondó/makrí	*It is too big/small/ tight/short/long*
έχετε ένα μεγαλύτερο/μικρότερο; éhete éna meghalítero/mikrótero	*Have you a larger one/smaller one?*
Αυτό είναι εντάξει aftó íne endáksi	*This one fits*
Θα το πάρω tha to páro	*I will take it*
μ'αρέσει marési	*I like it*
Δεν μ'αρέσει then marési	*I don't like it*

b.

παπούτσια papóotsya	*shoes*
πέδιλα péthila	*sandals*
κάλτσες káltses	*socks, stockings*
καλσόν kalsón	*tights*

θέλω ένα ζευγάρι παπούτσια/πέδιλα
  thélo éna zevghári
  papoótsya/péthila — *I would like a pair of shoes/sandals*

Μ'αρέσουν marésoon — *I like them*

---

c. χρώμα hróma — *colour*
άσπρο/μαύρο áspro/mávro — *white/black*
γκρι gri — *grey*
κόκκινο/πράσινο kókino/prásino — *red/green*
μπλε/κίτρινο ble/kítrino — *blue/yellow*
καφέ kafé — *brown*

Τι χρώμα θέλετε; ti hróma thélete? — *What colour would you like?*

πιο ανοικτό pyo aniktó — *lighter*
πιο σκούρο pyo skoóro — *darker*

---

d. σαπούνι sapoóni — *soap*
σαμπουάν sampooán — *shampoo*
πετσέτα petséta — *towel*
οδοντόκρεμα othondókrema — *toothpaste*
οδοντόβουρτσα othondóvoortsa — *toothbrush*
ξυριστική μηχανή ksiristikí mihaní — *electric razor*
σερβιέτες υγείας serviétes iyías — *sanitary towels*
μαντήλι mandíli — *handkerchief*
κρέμα ηλίου kréma ilíoo — *suntan cream*
λάδι ηλίου láthi ilíoo — *suntan oil*
γυαλιά ηλίου yaliá ilíoo — *sunglasses*
χαρτομάντηλα hartomándila — *tissues*

e. ΚΟΜΜΩΤΗΡΙΟ κομμωτήριο komotírio — *hairdresser*

ΚΟΥΡΕΙΟ κουρείο koorío — *barber's*
τσατσάρα, κτένα tsatsára, kténa — *comb*

Μόνο λούσιμο. móno loósimo — *Shampoo only.*
Λούσιμο και μίζ-αν-πλί.
  loósimo ke mizanplí — *Shampoo and set.*
Μία μίζ-αν-πλί με το πιστολάκι.
  mía mizanplí me to pistoláki — *Blow-dry (set).*
Κόψιμο και ξύρισμα, παρακαλώ.
  Kópsimo ke ksírisma, parakaló — *Haircut and shave, please.*

Money and Shopping → 9

What are these called in Greek? Say you would like to buy
them, starting with **θέλω ν' αγοράσω** . . . thélo naghoráso (*I
would like to buy* . . .)

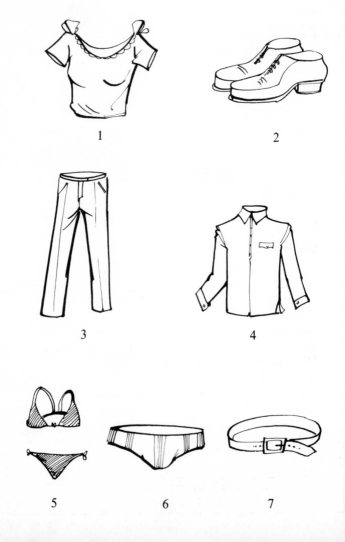

1

2

3

4

5   6   7

8 Say you would like to try it on.

9 Ask the assistant if she has anything bigger.

10 Say you will take it.

What are the following called in Greek? Ask the Chemist if he has them. Begin with ἔχετε . . . éhete (*Do you have . . .*)

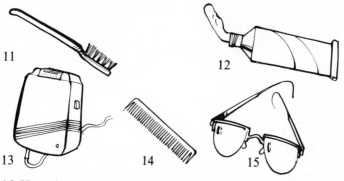

11

12

13

14

15

16 How do you say in Greek (*a*) I like it!
                                     (*b*) I like them!

- When buying **clothes** or **shoes**, remember that Greek sizes are different from British ones.

Shoe sizes

British	1	2	3	4	5	6	7	8	9	10	11	12
Greek	33	34–35	36	37	38	39–40	41	42	43	44	45	46

Dress sizes

British	10	12	14	16	18	20
Greek	42	44	46	48	50	52

Collar sizes

British	13	13½	14	14½	15	15½	16	16½	17
Greek	33	34	35–36	37	38	39	41	42	43

Suits, coats

British	36	38	40	42	44	46
Greek	46	48	50	52	54	56

20 Accidents and Emergencies

a. Car breakdown, Accidents **b.** Theft **c.** Police
d. Illness **e.** Chemist **f.** Doctor **g.** Help

a.
βλάβη vlávi	*breakdown*
δυστύχημα **th**istíhima	*accident*
σύγκρουση síngroosi	*collision* (formal)
τρακάρισμα trakárisma	*collision* (colloquial)
γκαράζ garáz	*garage*
ασφάλεια asfália	*insurance*

ΤΗΛΕΦΩΝΟ ΒΟΗΘΕΙΑΣ ΑΤΥΧΗΜΑΤΩΝ tiléfono voithías atihimáton	*emergency service telephone*
Έγινε ένα δυστύχημα éyine éna **th**istíhima	*There has been an accident.*
Δεν φταίω εγώ then ftéo eghó	*It's not my fault.*
Που είναι ένα γκαράζ; poo íne éna garáz	*Where is there a garage?*
Το αυτοκίνητο μου έχει μία βλάβη. to aftokínito moo éhi mía vlávi	*My car has broken down.*

b.
κλοπή klopí	*robbery, theft*
ΤΜΗΜΑ ΑΠΟΛΕΣΘΕΝΤΩΝ tmíma apolesthéndon	*Lost property*

Έχασα τα κλειδιά μου éhasa ta kli**th**yá moo	*I've lost my keys.*
μου έκλεψαν το πορτοφόλι μου/τα λεφτά μου/το αυτοκίνητο μου moo éklepsan to portofóli moo/ ta leftá moo/to aftokínito moo.	*Someone has stolen my wallet (purse)/ my money/my car*

c.
ΑΣΤΥΝΟΜΙΑ αστυνομία astinomía	*police*
δικηγόρος **th**ikighóros	*lawyer*

Τηλεφωνείστε γρήγορα στην αστυνομία! tilefoníste ghríghora stin astinomía	*Call the police immediately!*
Θέλω ένα διερμηνέα thélo éna **th**ierminéa	*I would like an interpreter.*

d. άρρωστος árostos — *ill, sick*
ηλίαση ilíasi — *sunstroke*

Είμαι άρρωστος.	íme árostos	*I am ill.*
Μ' έκαψε ο ήλιος.	mékapse o ílyos	*I have sunburn.*
Έχω πονοκέφαλο.	ého ponokéfalo	*I have a headache.*
Πονάει το στομάχι μου.	ponái to stomáhi moo	*I have stomach ache.*
Έχω πονόδοντο.	ého ponóthondo	*I have toothache.*
Έχω πυρετό.	ého piretó	*I have a fever.*
Τραυματίστηκα.	travmatístika	*I am injured.*

e. ΦΑΡΜΑΚΕΙΟ φαρμακείο — *chemist*
farmakío
φάρμακο fármako — *medicine*
αλοιφή alifí — *cream, ointment*
χάπι hápi — *pill*
τσιρότο tsiróto — *sticking plaster*
επίδεσμος epíthesmos — *bandage*

Που είναι ένα φαρμακείο;	poo íne éna farmakío	*Where is there a chemist?*
Μερικούς επιδέσμους, παρακαλώ.	merikoós epithésmoos, parakaló	*Some bandages, please.*

f. γιατρός yatrós — *doctor*
οδοντογιατρός othondoyatrós — *dentist*
νοσοκομείο nosokomío — *hospital*
ασθενοφόρο asthenofóro — *ambulance*

Γρήγορα ένα γιατρό!	ghríghora éna yatró	*Quick, a doctor!*
Καλέστε ένα ασθενοφόρο.	kaléste éna asthenofóro	*Call an ambulance.*
Δέν είναι τίποτα το σοβαρό.	then íne típota to sovaró	*It's nothing serious.*

g. κίνδυνος kínthinos — *danger*
ΠΡΟΣΟΧΗ προσοχή prosohí — *attention! look out!*
Βοήθεια! voíthia — *Help!*

ΕΞΟΔΟΣ ΚΙΝΔΥΝΟΥ	*Emergency Exit*
éksothos kinthínoo	

20   Accidents and Emergencies

1 You are telephoning a garage. Tell the mechanic that your car has broken down.

2 You are involved in an accident. How do you ask someone to call the police?

3 How do you say there has been an accident?

4 You were not to blame for the accident. What do you tell the police?

5 Tell the police you have lost your wallet/purse.

6 Say that someone has stolen your car.

7 You have witnessed an accident. How do you ask someone to call an ambulance?

8 You are not feeling well and go to the doctor. Tell him you have:
   (a) a headache.
   (b) toothache.
   (c) a fever.
   (d) sunburn.

9 The doctor does not think it is serious. What does he say?

10 Ask the chemist for:
   (a) some ointment.
   (b) some sticking plasters.
   (c) some medicine.

11 You are locked inside a building. What do you shout through the window?

12 The main exit is blocked. What sign do you look for?

- **The breakdown service** is free to foreign visitors who are members of the national Automobile or Touring Clubs in their own country. Otherwise, road assistance is offered to foreign motorists, provided they join ELPA (Greek Road Assistance Service) on the spot and pay a registration fee together with one year's subscription.

- Useful **Emergency telephones:**
  ELPA Road Assistance No: 104
  Athens First Aid Station No: 166
  Fire Brigade No: 199
  Coastguard Emergency Patrol No: 108
  Tourist Police No: 171

- **Medical Care. Urgent cases** requiring immediate hospital treatment are handled by the roster of hospitals which take in such cases day and night. Tel: 166.

  A visit to a **private doctor** is quite expensive and the bill must be settled immediately.

- If a chemist is shut, you will usually find a list of chemists open at nights and on Sundays displayed on its door. Chemists in Greece can be recognised by their red cross.

- Most Greek doctors speak English or know the language well enough to meet your needs, but here is a list of some useful words and expressions:

Φαρμακείο	*Chemist*
Γιατρός	*Doctor*
Νοσοκόμα	*Nurse*
έχω ένα πόνο εδώ.	*I have a pain here.*
με δάγκασε ένα έντομο.	*I was bitten by an insect.*
αισθάνομαι ζάλη.	*I am dizzy.*
έχω τάση γιά εμετό.	*I feel sick.*
έχω δυσπεψία.	*I have indigestion.*
έχω κράμπα.	*I have cramp.*
χρειάζομαι ένα φάρμακο.	*I need some medicine.*
τι σας οφείλω;	*How much do I owe you?*

Answers

1 General Expressions

1 Γειά σου (yásoo). 2 Πολύ καλά, ευχαριστώ (polí kalá efharistó). 3 Αντίο (andío). 4 Καλησπέρα (kalispéra). 5 Ναι, παρακαλώ (ne parakaló). 6 Όχι, ευχαριστώ (óhi efharistó). 7 Το διαβατήριο σας, παρακαλώ (to **thi**avatírio sas, parakaló). 8 Είμαι η κυρία Σμιθ (íme i kiría "smith"). 9 Ναι, αυτή είναι η βαλίτσα μου (ne aftí íne i valítsa moo). 10 Όχι, αυτή δεν είναι η βαλίτσα μου (óhi aftí then íne i valítsa moo). 11 Με συγχωρείτε (me sinhoríte).

2 Arriving in Greece

1 Βαλίτσα (valítsa). 2 Τσάντα (tsánta). 3 Έλεγχος διαβατηρίου (élenhos **thi**avatiríoo). 4 Το διαβατήριο σας, παρακαλώ (to **thi**avatírio sas parakaló). 5 Με λένε... (me léne). 6 Ναι, είμαι Άγγλος (*if a man*) (ne íme ánglos). Ναι, είμαι Αγγλίδα (*if a woman*) (ne íme anglí**tha**). 7 Τίποτα για δήλωση (típota ya **th**ílosi). 8 Ανοίξτε τη βαλίτσα σας, παρακαλώ (aníkste ti valítsa sas parakaló). 9 Καλό ταξίδι! (kaló taksí**thi**). 10 Μεγάλη Βρετανία (megh9áli vretanía). 11 Ηνωμένες Πολιτείες (Αμερική) (inoménes políties (amerikí)). 12 Αυστραλία (afstralía). 13 Έχετε μία αγγλική εφημερίδα; (éhete mía anglikí efimerí**tha**).

3 Driving a Car

1 Αυτοκίνητο (aftokínito). 2 Τροχόσπιτο (trohóspito). 3 Πόση βενζίνη θέλετε; (pósi venzíni (**th**élete)). 4 Γεμάτο, παρακαλώ (yemáto parakaló). 5 Ελέγξτε το λάδι, παρακαλώ (elénkste to lá**thi** parakaló). 6 Απαγορεύεται η στάθμευση (apaghorévete i státhmefsi). 7 Εθνική οδός (ethnikí o**thós**). 8 Πρατήριο βενζίνης (pratírio venzínis). 9 Διόδια (**thió**thia). 10 Τελωνείο (telonío).

4 Finding your Way

1 Ένα χάρτη της Ελλάδας, παρακαλώ (éna hárti tis elá**thas** parakaló). 2 Ένα χάρτη της πόλης, παρακαλώ (éna hárti tis pólis parakaló). 3 Που είναι η οδός Αθηνάς; (poo íne i o**thós** athinás). 4 Στρίψετε δεξιά (strípsete **th**eksyá). 5 Αριστερά (aristerá). 6 Δεξιά (**th**eksyá). 7 Ευθεία (efthía). 8 Που είναι η στάση, παρακαλώ; (poo íne i stási parakaló). 9 Είναι μακριά; (íne makriá). 10 Ευθεία, στό δεύτερο στενό δεξιά (efthía sto **th**éftero stenó **th**eksyá). 11 Θεσσαλονίκη (thessaloníki) Αλεξανδρούπολη (aleksan**thr**oópoli) Λάρισα, (lárisa), Λαμία (lamía), Λιβαδειά (livathyá), Αθήνα (athína), Κόρινθος (kórinthos), Πάτρα (pátra), Άργος (árghos), Τρίπολη (trípoli), Καλαμάτα (kalamáta).

5 Public Transport

1 Στο αεροδρόμιο, παρακαλώ (sto aerothrómio parakaló). 2
ΠΛΗΡΟΦΟΡΙΕΣ (plirofories). 3 ΔΕΞΙΑ (theksyá). 4 φεριμπότ
(feribót). 5 Βαπόρι (vapóri). 6 Στο Πειραιά (sto pireá). 7 Είσοδος
(ísothos). 8 Ένα εισιτήριο για την Αθήνα, παρακαλώ (éna isitírio
ya tin athína parakaló). 9 Ένα εισιτηριο με επιστροφή (éna
isitírio me epistrofí).

6 Accommodation

1 Κρεβάτι (kreváti). 2 Κλειδί (klithí). 3 Υπάρχει ένα ξενοδοχείο
εδώ κοντά; (ipárhi éna ksenothohío ethó kondá). 4 Έχετε ένα
δωμάτιο, παρακαλώ; (éhete éna thomátio parakaló). 5 Ένα
δωμάτιο με ντους (éna thomátio me doos). 6 Πόσο κοστίζει;
(póso kostízi). 7 Τιμή δωματίου (timí thomatíoo). 8 ΙΣ (ισόγειο)
(isóyio). 9 Θέλω να πληρώσω (thélo na pliróso). 10 Που είναι η
τουαλέττα; (poo íne i tooaléta). 11 Ανδρών (anthrón).
12 Γυναικών (yinekón).

7 Numbers, Weights and Measures

1 Δεκα-πέντε (thekapénde). 2 Δεκα-εφτά (thekaeftá). 3 Εκατό
τριάντα δύο (ekató triánda thío). 4 Διακόσια έξη (thiakósia éksi).
5 Κοστίζει ενενήντα δραχμές (Kostízi enenínda thrahmés).
6 Κοστίζει πενήντα δραχμές (kostízi penínda thrahmés).
7 Κοστίζει εβδομήντα δραχμές (kostízi evthomínda thrahmés).
8 Κοστίζει ογδόντα δραχμές (kostízi oghthónda thrahmés).
9 Κοστίζει εκατόν εβδομήντα δραχμές (kostízi ekatón
evthomínda thrahmés). 10 Εβδομήντα δύο χιλιόμετρα
(evthomínda thío hilyómetra). Διακόσια δεκα-πέντε χιλιόμετρα
(thiakósia thekapénde hilyómetra). Τριακόσια πενήντα έξη
χιλιόμετρα (triakósia penínda éksi hilyómetra). Πεντακόσια οχτώ
χιλιόμετρα (pendakósia ohtó hilyómetra). Πεντακόσια πενήντα
χιλιόμετρα (pendakósia penínda hilyómetra). Ογδόντα τρία
χιλιόμετρα (oghthónda tría hilyómetra). Διακόσια δεκα-τρία
χιλιόμετρα (thiakósia thekatría hilyómetra). 11 Ένα κιλό
ντομάτες (éna kiló domátes). 12 Τρία κιλά μήλα (tría kilá míla).
13 Ένα λίτρο μεταλλικό νερό (éna lítro metalikó neró).

8 Times and Dates

1 Πρωί (proí). 2 Απόγευμα (apóyevma). 3 Νύχτα (níhta).
4 Εξήντα λεπτά (eksínda leptá) = Μία ώρα (mía óra). 5 Είκοσι
τέσσερις ώρες (íkosi téseris óres). 6 Εφτά μέρες (eftá
méres) = Μία εβδομάδα (mía evthomátha). 7 Τι ώρα είναι; (ti
óra íne). 8 Είναι μία, η ωρα (íne mía i óra). 9 Είναι δύο το
απόγευμα (íne thío to apóyevma). 10 Είναι έξη το βράδυ (íne éksi
to vráthi). 11 Πότε φεύγετε; (nóte févyete). 12 Φεύγω αύριο το
πρωί στις οχτώ (févgho ávrio to proí stis ohtó). 13 Εννιά και
πέντε (enyá ke pénde). Δέκα και δέκα (théka ke théka). Ένδεκα

και είκοσι (éntheka ke íkosi). Δώδεκα η ώρα (thótheka i óra).
Δώδεκα και σαράντα πέντε (thótheka ke saránda pénde).
14 (a) σε είκοσι λεπτά (se íkosi leptá). (b) σε μισή ώρα (se misí
óra). (c) σε δέκα μέρες (se théka méres). (d) σε έξη μήνες (se éksi
mínes).

9 Money and Shopping

1 Τράπεζα (trápeza). 2 Τι θέλετε; (ti thélete). 3 Θέλω να δω
πρώτα (thélo na tho próta). 4 Πόσο κοστίζει αυτό το βάζο; (póso
kostízi aftó to vázo). 5 Κοστίζει χίλιες δραχμές (kostízi hilies
thrahmés). 6 Είναι πολύ ακριβό; (íne polí akrivó). 7 Θέλετε
τίποτε άλλο; (thélete tipote álo). 8 Όχι, ευχαριστώ (óhi
efharistó). 9 Ειδική προσφορά (ithikí prosforá). 10 Κλειστό
(klistó). 11 Ταμείο (tamío). 12 Εκατό δώδεκα δραχμές (ekató
thótheka thrahmés). 13 Είκοσι τέσσερις δραχμές (íkosi téseris
thrahmés). Τριάντα έξη δραχμές (triánda éksi thrahmés). Είκοσι
πέντε δραχμές (íkosi pénde thrahmés). Είκοσι εφτά δραχμές
(íkosi eftá thrahmés).

10 Meals

1 (a) Πρωινό (proinó). (b) Γεύμα (yévma). (c) Δείπνο (thípno).
2 (a) Ένα φλιτζάνι καφέ (éna flijáni kafé). (b) Ένα ποτήρι (éna
potíri). (c) Ένα μπουκάλι κρασί (éna bookáli krasí). (d) Ένα
πηρούνι (éna piroóni). (e) Ένα πιάτο (éna pyáto). (f) Ένα
μαχαίρι (éna mahéri). (g) Ένα κουτάλι (éna kootáli). 3 Σουβλάκι
(soovláki). 4 Τυρόπιτα (tirópita). 5 Ντολμάδες (dolmáthes).
6 Γιαούρτι (yaoórti).

11 Restaurants

1 (a) στο ζαχαροπλαστείο (sto zaharoplastío). (b) στο
εστιατόριο/στη ταβέρνα (sto estiatório/sti tavérna). (c) στο μπάρ
(sto bar). 2 Είναι αυτή η καρέκλα ελεύθερη, παρακαλώ; (íne aftí i
karékla eléftheri parakaló). 3 Θέλω κάτι να φάω (thélo káti na
fáo). 4 Τον κατάλογο, παρακαλώ (ton katálogho parakaló).
5 Μου δίνετε το αλάτι, παρακαλώ (moo thínete to aláti parakaló).
6 Τι θέλετε να πιείτε; (ti thélete na pyíte). 7 Θέλω να πληρώσω.
Τον λογαριασμό, παρακαλώ (thélo na pliróso ton loghariasmó
parakaló). 8 Περιλαμβάνεται το φιλοδώρημα; (perilamvánete to
filothórima). 9 Εντάξει; (endáksi). 10 Αλάτι (aláti). 11 Πιπέρι
(pipéri).

12 Starters, Meat, Fish

1 Σούπα ημέρας (soópa iméras). 2 Φιλέτο (filéto). 3 Αρνάκι
(arnáki). 4 Ομελέττα (omeléta). 5 Ψάρι (psári). 6 Ψάρι τηγανητό
(psári tighanitó). 7 Ψάρι στη σχάρα (psári sti shára).
8 Μπιφτέκι/φιλέτο (biftéki/filéto). 9 Κοτόπουλο (kotópoolo).
10 Ψάρι (psári). 11 Μουσακά(ς) (moosaká(s)).

13 Vegetables, Fruit, Desserts

1 Μ'αρέσει το καρπούζι (marési to karpoózi). 2 Μ'αρέσουν τα σταφύλια (marésoon ta stafílya). 3 Μ'αρέσει το μήλο (marési to mílo). 4 Μ'αρέσει το πορτοκάλι (marési to portokáli). 5 Μ'αρέσει το λεμόνι (marési to lemóni). 6 Μ'αρέσουν οι πατάτες (marésoon i patátes). 7 Μ'αρέσουν τα καρότα (marésoon ta karóta). 8 Μ'αρέσει η ντομάτα (marési i domáta). 9 Μ'άρέσει η μελιτζάνα (marési i melidzána). 10 Γλυκά (ghliká). 11 (a) ένα μπακλαβά, παρακαλώ (éna baklavá parakaló). (b) ένα παγωτό, παρακαλώ (éna paghotó parakaló). (c) ένα πορτοκάλι, παρακαλώ (éna portokáli parakaló).

14 Drinking and Smoking

1 Μία πορτοκαλάδα, παρακαλώ (mía portokalátha parakaló). 2 Μία λεμονάδα, παρακαλώ (mía lemonátha parakaló). 3 Μία κόκα-κόλα (mía kóka-kóla). 4 Δύο καφέδες Νές (thío kaféthes nes). 5 Ένα τσάι με γάλα (éna tsái me ghála). 6 Μία μπύρα (mía bíra). 7 Ένα μπουκάλι κόκκινο κρασί (éna bookáli kókino krasí). 8 Ένα ποτήρι νερό (éna potíri neró). 9 Ένα ούζο (éna oózo). 10 Τσιγάρα (tsighára). 11 Αναπτήρας (anaptíras). 12 Τιρμπουσόν (tirboosón).

15 Sightseeing and Entertainment

1 Η πύλη των λεόντων στις Μυκήνες (i píli ton leóndon stis mikínes) (*Lion's Gate at Mycenae*). 2 Ο Δίας (o **th**ías) (*Zeus*). 3 Ο Ερμής του Πραξιτέλους (o ermís too praksitéloos) (*Hermes by Praxiteles*). 4 Η είσοδος σταδίου της Ολυμπίας (i ísothos stathíoo tis olimbías) (*Entrance to the Stadium at Olympia*). 5 Ένα εισιτήριο, παρακαλώ (éna isitírio parakaló). 6 Πόσο κοστίζει η είσοδος; (póso kostízi i íso**th**os).

16 Excursions and Recreation

1 Βλέπω το νησί "Μύκονος" (vlépo to nisí míkonos) (*Mykonos*). 2 Βλέπω τον Ισθμό της Κορίνθου (vlépo ton isthmó tis korínthoo) (*Isthmus of Corinth*). 3 Βλέπω δύο δελφίνια (vlépo **th**ío **th**elfínya) (*dolphins*). 4 (a) ΠΛΑΖ (plaz). (b) ΠΙΣΙΝΑ (pisína). 5 Ομπρέλλα ηλίου (ombréla ilíoo). 6 Πολυθρόνα (polithróna). 7 Στρώμα φουσκωτό (stróma fooskotó). 8 Θέλω ν' αγοράσω μία φωτογραφική μηχανή (thélo naghoráso mía fotoghrafikí mihaní). 9 Θέλω ν' αγοράσω ένα φίλμ (thélo naghoráso éna film). 10 (a) θέλω να νοικιάσω ένα κανώ (thélo na nikyáso éna kanó). (b) θέλω να νοικιάσω μία βάρκα (thélo na nikyáso mía várka).

17 The Weather

1 Είναι ασταθής (íne astathís). 2 Είναι ασταθής (íne astathís). 3 Είναι συννεφιά (íne sinefyá). 4 Βρέχει και κάνει κρύο (vréhi ke káni krío). 5 Ο ήλιος λάμπει και κάνει ζέστη (o ílyos lámbi ke

káni zésti). 6 Καλός καιρός (kalós kerós). 7 Άσχημος καιρός (áshimos kerós). 8 Άσχημος καιρός (áshimos kerós).

18 Post Office and Telephone

1 Κάρτα (kárta). 2 Γραμματοκιβώτιο (ghramatokivótio). 3 Φάκελος (fákelos). 4 Διεύθυνση (thiéfthinsi). 5 Γραμματόσημο (ghramatósimo). 6 Στυλό (stiló). 7 Πόσο κοστίζει μία κάρτα για την Αγγλία; (póso kostízi mía kárta ya tin anglía). 8 Μερικά γραμματόσημα, παρακαλώ (meriká ghramatósima parakaló). 9 Τηλέφωνο (tiléfono). 10 Τηλεφωνικός κατάλογος (tilefonikós katáloghos).

19 Clothing and Toiletries

1 Θέλω ν' αγοράσω μία μπλούζα (thélo naghoráso mía blóoza). 2 Θέλω ν' αγοράσω παπούτσια (thélo naghoráso papóotsya). 3 Θέλω ν' αγοράσω ένα πανταλόνι (thélo naghoráso éna pantalóni). 4 Θέλω ν' αγοράσω ένα πουκάμισο (thélo naghoráso éna pookámiso). 5 Θέλω ν' αγοράσω ένα μπικίνι (thélo naghoráso éna bikíni). 6 Θέλω ν' αγοράσω ένα μαγιό (thélo naghoráso éna mayó). 7 Θέλω ν' αγοράσω μία ζώνη (thélo naghoráso mía zóni). 8 Μπορώ να το δοκιμάσω; (boró na to thokimáso). 9 Έχετε ένα μεγαλύτερο; (éhete éna meghalítero). 10 Θα το πάρω (tha to páro). 11 Έχετε μία οδοντόβουρτσα, παρακαλώ; (éhete mía othondóvoortsa-parakalo). 12 Έχετε μία οδοντόκρεμα; (éhete mía othondókrema). 13 Έχετε μία ξυριστική μηχανή; (éhete mía ksiristikí mihaní). 14 Έχετε μία κτένα; (éhete mía kténa). 15 Έχετε γυαλιά ηλίου; (éhete yaliá ilíoo). 16 μ'αρέσει! (marési). μ'αρέσουν! (marésoon).

20 Accidents and Emergencies

1 Το αυτοκίνητο μου έχει μία βλάβη (to aftokínito moo éhi mía vlávi). 2 Τηλεφωνείστε γρήγορα στην Αστυνομία (tilefoníste ghríghora stin astinomía). 3 Έγινε ένα δυστύχημα (éyine éna thistíhima). 4 Δεν φταίω εγώ (then ftéo eghó). 5 Έχασα το πορτοφόλι μου (éhasa to portofóli moo). 6 Μου έκλεψαν το αυτοκίνητο (moo éklepsan to aftokínito). 7 Καλέστε ένα ασθενοφόρο (kaléste éna asthenofóro). 8 (a) έχω πονοκέφαλο (ého ponokéfalo). (b) έχω πονόδοντο (ého ponóthondo). (c) έχω πυρετό (ého piretó). (d) μ' έκαψε ο ήλιος (mékapse o ílyos). 9 Δεν είναι τίποτα το σοβαρό (then íne típota to sovaró). 10 (a) μία αλοιφή, παρακαλώ (mía alifí, parakaló). (b) μερικά τσιρότα (meriká tsiróta). (c) ένα φάρμακο (éna fármako). 11 Βοήθεια! (voíthia). 12 ΕΞΟΔΟΣ ΚΙΝΔΥΝΟΥ (éksothos kinthínoo).

VOCABULARY

Greek – English Vocabulary

In front of the Greek nouns whose gender cannot be determined by the ending -oς (= masculine), -α, -η (= feminine) or -o (= neuter), the corresponding articles o = the (masculine), η = the (feminine) or το = the (neuter), e.g. (o) Έλληνας, (η) δεσποινίς, (το) βράδυ, are put into parentheses.

(το) άγαλμα statue 15b
(η) Αγγλία England 2c
(o) Άγγλος English (man) 2c
(η) Αγγλίδα English (woman) 2c
αγγλικός English (adjective) 2c
(τα) αγγλικά English (language) 2c
(το) αγγούρι cucumber 13a
άγιος, αγία saint (male/female) 15b
αγκινάρες artichokes 13a
αγορά market 9c
(η) άδεια οδηγήσεως driver's licence 2b
(o) αέρας wind (colloquial) 17c
(η) ΑΔΙΕΞΟΔΟΣ No through road 3c
αεροδρόμιο, (o) αερολιμένας airport 5b
αεροπορικώς airmail 18b
αθώος innocent 20a
αίθουσα αναμονής waiting room 5a
αίθριος fair 17b
(o) ακτοφύλακας lifeguard 16c
ακτή coast 16b
ακριβό expensive 9d
(το) απόγευμα afternoon 8a
(το) αλάτι salt 11c
(οι) αλλοδαποί foreigners 2c
αλοιφή cream, ointment 20e
(η) Αμερική America (U.S.A.) 2c
(o) Αμερικάνος American (man) 2c
(η) Αμερικανίδα American (woman) 2c
αμερικάνικος American (adjective) 2c
(η) άμμος sand 16c
αμύγδαλα almonds 13b
αμφιθέατρο amphitheatre 15b
(o) αμφορέας amphora 15b
(o) αναπτήρας lighter 14c
(οι) ΑΝΑΧΩΡΗΣΕΙΣ departure (times) 5e
(τα) αναψυκτικά refreshments 14a

ΑΝΔΡΩΝ MEN's (toilet) 6d
άνεμος wind (formal) 17c
αντίο goodbye 1b
(o) άντρας husband 1f
(η) απόδειξη receipt 11d
ΑΝΟΙΚΤΟ open 9c
ΑΠΑΓΟΡΕΥΕΤΑΙ It is forbidden 3d
(το) απόγευμα afternoon 8b
(οι) αποσκευές luggage 2a
αρέσει (μ' αρέσει) I like (it) or μ' αρέσουν I like (them) 19b
αριθμός number 7b
αριστερά left 4d
(το) αρνάκι lamb 12b
(το) αρνί mutton 12b
άρρωστος ill, sick 20d
ΑΡΧΑΙΑ ΚΟΡΙΝΘΟΣ Old Corinth 4b
αρχαιολογικός τόπος archaeological site 15b
(τα) αρχαία antiquities 15b
αρχαία ελληνική τραγωδία classical Greek tragedy 15b
(το) ασανσέρ lift 6b
ασθενοφόρο ambulance 20f
άσπρο white 19c
αστάθεια changeable weather 17c
αστακός lobster 12d
αστυνομία police 20c
ασφάλεια insurance 20a
άσχημος καιρός bad weather 17c
(τα) άτομα people (pl.) 6b
αυγό egg 12c
αύριο tomorrow 8b, 17a
αυτό είναι για σας this is for you 11d
(η) Αυστραλία Australia 2c
(o) Αυστραλός Australian (man) 2c
(η) Αυστραλέζα Australian (woman) 2c
αυτοκινητάμαξα railcar 5a

Greek – English Vocabulary

αυτοκίνητο car 3a
αυτός this 1e
(οι) ΑΦΙΞΕΙΣ arrival (times) 5e
Αχθοφόρε! Porter! 5d
αχλάδια pears 13b

βαλίτσα suitcase 2a
βάζο vase 9c
βάρκα rowing boat 16c
βάρκα με μηχανή motor boat 16c
βάρκα με πανί sailing boat 16c
βαθειά deep 16d
βέβαια of course 11a
βενζίνη petrol 3c
βερύκοκα apricots 13b
βλάβη breakdown 20a
βοήθεια! help 20
βουνό mountain 16b
βούτυρο butter 10d
(το) βαπόρι steamer 5c
(το) βράδυ evening 8b
βρέχει it is raining 17c
βροχή rain 17c

(το) γάλα milk 14c
γαρίδα shrimp 12d
(το) γεύμα lunch 10a
Γειά σου hello/goodbye (informal) 1b
(το) γιαούρτι yoghurt 10d
για for 6b
για μία νύχτα for one night 6b
γιατρός doctor 20f
(το) γκαράζ garage 20a
(το) γκαρσόν waiter 11d
γκρι grey 19c
(τα) γλυκά desserts, sweets 13c
(το) γράμμα letter 18b
(τα) γραμματόσημα stamps 18b
γραμματοκιβώτιο mailbox 18b
γραμμή track 5a
Γραφείο Τουρισμού Tourist Office 15a
γραφείο αποσκευών left luggage office 5a
γρήγορα quickly 20c, 20f

(τα) γυαλιά ηλίου sunglasses 19d
(η) γυναίκα wife, 1f
ΓΥΝΑΙΚΩΝ WOMEN's (toilet) 6e
γύρος tour (colloq.) 16a

δείπνο dinner 10a
δέκα ten 7a
(το) δελφίνι dolphin 16b
(τα) ΔΕΜΑΤΑ parcels 18b
δεξιά right 4d
(η) δεσποινίς Miss 1d
Δευτέρα Monday 8c
ΔΗΛΩΣΗ (ΕΙΔΗ ΓΙΑ ΔΗΛΩΣΗ goods to declare) 2a
διερμηνέα(ς) interpreter 20c
διαβατήριο passport 2b
διακόσια two hundred 7a
(η) διεύθυνση address 2b, 18b
δικηγόρος lawyer 20c
(τά) διόδια toll 3b
διπλό δωμάτιο double room 6b
(τα) δοκιμαστήρια changing rooms 19a
(τα) δολλάρια dollars 9a
(το) δράμα drama 15c
δραχμή drachma 9a
(τα) ΔΡΟΜΟΛΟΓΙΑ timetables 5e
δρόμος road 3b
δύο two 7a
δροσιά cool (weather) 17d
(το) δυστύχημα accident 20a
δώδεκα twelve 7a
δωμάτιο room 6b

εβδομάδα week 8c
εβδομήντα seventy 7a
έγινε.... there has been.... 20a
εγώ I 1b
έγχρωμο φίλμ colour film 16d
εδώ here 4d
(η) εθνική οδός motorway 3b
(η) ειδική προσφορά special offer 9c
εικόνα icon 15b
είκοσι twenty 7a

Greek – English Vocabulary

ίμαι I am 1d
τα) ΕΙΣΙΤΗΡΙΑ tickets 5e
ισιτήριο ticket 15d
ισιτήριο με επιστροφή a return
  ticket 5e
η) είσοδος entrance 5d
ΞΙΣΟΔΟΣ ΕΛΕΥΘΕΡΑ admission
  free 15d
κατό (one) hundred 7a
κδρομή excursion 16a
κεί there 4d
η) έκθεση exhibition 15b
κεί πέρα over there 6d
κκλησία church 15b
ΕΛΕΓΧΟΣ ΔΙΑΒΑΤΗΡΙΟΥ pass-
  port control 2b
οι) ελιές olives 13a
η) Ελλάδα Greece 2c
ο) Έλληνας Greek (man) 2c
η) Ελληνίδα Greek (woman) 2c
ελληνικός Greek (adjective) 2c
τα) Ελληνικά Greek (language) 2c
εμπρός hello? 18c
ένα one 7a
ένας, μία, ένα a, an 1e
ένδεκα eleven 7a
ενενήντα ninety 7a
εννιά nine 7a
εννιακόσια nine hundred 7a
ενοικιάσεις αυτοκινήτων car rental
  3a
Εντάξει! It's all right 1a; keep the
  change 11d
εξακόσια six hundred 7a
εξήντα sixty 7a
έξι six 7a
η) έξοδος exit 5d
ΕΞΟΔΟΣ ΚΙΝΔΥΝΟΥ emergency
  exit 20g
επίδεμος bandage 20e
εσείς you (formal) 1f
εσπρέσσο espresso 14a
ΕΣΤΙΑΤΟΡΙΟ restaurant 11a
ευθεία straight ahead 4d
ευκαιρία bargain 9c
ευχαριστώ! thank you 1c
εφτά seven 7a
εφτακόσια seven hundred 7a

έχετε καθόλου.... have you got
  any.... 9a

ζακέτα jacket 19a
ζάχαρη sugar 11c
ΖΑΧΑΡΟΠΛΑΣΤΕΙΟ pastry
  shop 11a
ζέστη (κάνει ζέστη it is warm/hot)
  17b
(το) ζευγάρι pair 19b
ζώνη belt 19a

ήλιος sun 17b
ηλίαση sunstroke 20d
ημερομηνία date 2b
ήρεμη calm (sea) 17c

θάλασσα sea 16b
θαλασσινά shellfish 10e
θαλάσσιο σκί water-skiing 16c
θέατρο theatre 15b
Θέλω.... I would like.... 14a
Θέλετε.... Would you like.... 10c
θερμοκρασία temperature 17a
ΘΕΣΗ seat 5e
θύελλα storm 17c

ισθμός isthmus 16b
ισόγειο ground floor 6b

καθαρός clean 16c, clear 17b
καιρός weather 17a
καλά well 1b
(τα) καλαμαράκια squid 12d
Καλημέρα! good morning 1b
Καληνύχτα good night 1b
Καλησπέρα! good evening! 1b
καλός καιρός good weather 17b
(το) καλσόν tights 19b
(οι) κάλτσες socks, stockings 19b
(το) κάμπινγκ campsite 6a
Κάνει ζέστη It is warm/hot 17b
(ο) Καναδάς Canada 2c
(ο) Καναδός Canadian (man) 2c
(η) Καναδέζα Canadian (woman) 2c

Greek – English Vocabulary

(το) **κανώ** canoe 16d
καπέλο hat 19a
καπουτσίνο cappuccino 14a
(το) **καράβι** boat 5c
(οι) **καραβίδες** crayfish 12d
καρέκλα chair 11a
(τα) **καρότα** carrots 13a
(το) **καρπούζι** watermelon 13b
κάρτα postcard 18b
(τα) **καρύδια** walnuts 13b
(ο) **καρχαρίας** shark 16b
καταιγίδα thunderstorm 17c
(οι) **κατακόμβες** catacombs 15b
κατάλογος menu, 11b
(το) **κατάστημα** store 9c
(το) **κατσικάκι** kid (young goat) 12b
καφέ brown 19c
ΚΑΦΕΝΕΙΟ café 11a
(ο) **καφέ(ς)** coffee 10c, 14a
(το) **κέικ** cake 13c
ΚΕΝΤΡΙΚΟΣ ΛΙΜΗΝ ΠΕΙΡΑΙΩΣ
  Central harbour of Piraeus 5c
κέντρο town centre 4b
(τα) **κεράσια** cherries 13b
(το) **κέρμα** coin 9a
(οι) **κεφτέδες** meatballs 12b
κιθάρα guitar 15c
κι εσείς; and you? (formal) 1b
κι εσύ; and you? (informal) 1b
κιλό kilogram 7b
κίνδυνος danger 20g
κινηματογράφος cinema 15b
κίτρινο yellow 19c
(το) **κλειδί** key 6b
ΚΛΕΙΣΤΟ closed 8c, 9c
κλινάμαξα sleeping car 5a
κγοπή robbery, theft 20b
κόκα-κόλα coca-cola 14a
κόκκινο red 19c
(τα) **κολοκυθάκια** courgettes 13a
κόλπος gulf 16b
(το) **κολύμπι** swimming 16d
κολυμπώ I swim 16c
κολώνα column 15b
(το) **κονιάκ** cognac 14b
κομμωτήριο hairdresser 19e
κοστίζει (it) costs 6c, 9d, 8b
κότα chicken 12c

κοτόπουλο young chicken 12c
κοτόσουπα chicken soup 12a
(το) **κουνουπίδι** cauliflower 13a
ΚΟΥΡΕΙΟ Barber's 19e
(το) **κουτάλι** spoon 10b
(το) **κρασί** wine 14b
κρασί γλυκό sweet wine 14b
κρασί κόκκινο red wine 14b
κρασί άσπρο white wine 14b
κρασί ξηρό dry wine 14b
(το) **κρέας** meat 12b
(το) **κρεβάτι** bed 6b
(η) **κρέμα ηλίου** suntan cream 19d
(τα) **κρεμμύδια** onions 13a
ΚΡΕΟΠΩΛΕΙΟ butcher's shop 10e
κρύο cold (weather) 17d
κυματώδης very rough (sea) 17c
κυρία Mrs., 1d
Κυριακή Sunday 8c
κύριος gentleman; Mr., 1d
κωμωδία comedy 15c

(το) **λάδι** oil 3c, 11c
λάδι ηλίου suntan oil 19d
λαϊκός χορός folk dancing 15c
λάχανο cabbage 13a
(τα) **λαχανικά** vegetables 13a
λάμπει (ο ήλιος λάμπει the sun i
  shining) 17b
λεμονάδα lemonade 14a
(το) **λεμόνι** lemon 13b
λέξη word 18d
λεπτό minute, 8a
(τα) **λεφτά** money 9a
λεωφορείο bus 5d
(η) **λεωφόρος** avenue 4c
λιακάδα sunshine 17b
λίρα (English) pound 9b
λίγο a little 7b
(το) **λικέρ** liqueur 14b
(το) **λιμάνι, (ο) λιμήν** harbour 5c
λίτρο litre 7b
λογαριασμό(ς) bill 6c, 11d
(τα) **λουκάνικα** hot dog 10d
(οι) **λουκουμάδες** doughnuts with
  honey 13c

Greek – English Vocabulary

(το) μαγιό bathing suit/trunks 19a
(το) μαντήλι handkerchief 19d
μαρμελάδα marmalade 10c
μαρούλι lettuce 13a
μαύρο black 19c
(το) μαχαίρι knife 10b
(το) μέγεθος size 19a
(οι) μεζέδες snacks 10d, starters 12a
μελιτζάνα aubergine 13a
μελιτζάνες γεμιστές stuffed auber-
 gines 13a
(το) MENOY complete, fixed price
 meal 11b
Μένω στην Αθήνα I live/stay in
 Athens 4b
(οι) ΜΕΖΕΔΕΣ starters 12a
με συγχωρείτε excuse me 1d
μέρα day 8b
(το) μεσημέρι noon 8b
(η) Μεσόγειος θάλασσα Mediterranean Sea 16b
μεταλλικό νερό mineral water 14a
(τα) μέτρα metres 7b
μέτριο medium 12b
(το) μηδέν zero 7a
Μη καπνίζετε! No smoking 14c
μήλο apple 13b
μηλόπιτα apple pie 13c
(ο) μήνας month 8c
μία a, an 1a, one 7a
μιλκ σέϊκ milk shake 14a
μονό δωμάτιο single room 6b
(το) μοναστήρι monastery 15b
μονόδρομος one-way traffic 3b
(το) μοσχάρι beef 12b
(το) μοσχαράκι veal 12b
μουσακά(ς) moussaka 12b
μουσείο museum 15b
μπακαλιάρος cod 12d
(ο) μπακλαβά(ς) baklava (pastry
 filled with nuts and honey) 13c
(οι) μπάμιες ladies' fingers 13a
μπάνιο bath 6b
(το) ΜΠΑΡ bar 11a
(το) μπαρμπούνι red mullet 12d
μπαταρία battery 16d
(τα) μπιζέλια peas 13a
(το) μπικίνι bikini 19b

(τα) μπισκότα biscuits 10c, 13c
μπλε blue 19c
μπλούζα blouse 19a
Μπορώ να may I? 18c
(οι) μπριζόλες chops 12b
(το) μπουζούκι bouzouki 15c
(το) μπουκάλι bottle 10b
μπύρα beer 14b

ναι yes 1a
ναός temple, 15b
NEA new 4b
νερό water 3b, 10b, 14a
(το) νησί island 16b
νοσοκομείο hospital 20f
ντήζελ diesel 3c
(η) ντισκοτέκ discothèque 15c
(οι) ντολμάδες vine leaves 10d
(ν)τομάτα tomato 13a
(ν)τομάτες γεμιστές stuffed tomatoes 13a
(ν)τοματόσουπα tomato soup 12a
(ν)τοματοσαλάτα tomato salad 13a
(το) ντους shower 6b
νύχτα night 8b
νυχτερινό κέντρο night club 15c

ξεναγός (tourist) guide 15d
ΞΕΝΟΔΟΧΕΙΟ hotel 6a
ξυριστική μηχανή electric razor 19d
ξηρό κρασί dry wine 14b

ο, η, το the 1e
ο … μου my 1f
ο … σας your 1f
ογδόντα eighty 7a
οδηγός driver 3a
(η) οδική κυκλοφορία traffic 3a
(ο) οδικός χάρτης road map 4a
οδοντόβουρτσα toothbrush 19d
οδοντογιατρός dentist 20f
οδοντόκρεμα toothpaste 19d
(η) οδός street 4c
ομελέττα omelette 12c
ομίχλη mist, fog 17d

Greek – English Vocabulary

ομπρέλλα ηλίου (beach) umbrella 16c
(το) όνομα name 2b
(τα) ορεκτικά starters 12a
ορίστε here you are! 1f
όροφος floor 6b
(η) Ουαλλία Wales 2c
(ο) Ουαλλός Welsh (man) 2c
(η) Ουαλλέζα Welsh (woman) 2c
ούζο ouzo 14b
όχι no 1a, 9b
οχτακόσια eight hundred 7a
οχτώ eight 7a

(ο) παγωμένο(ς) καφέ(ς) iced coffee 10c, 14a
(τα) παϊδάκια cutlets 12b
παγωτό ice cream 13c
πακέτο τσιγάρα pack of cigarettes 14c
(το) πανταλόνι trousers 19a
(τα) παπούτσια shoes 19b
παρακαλώ! please 1a, don't mention it 1c
παράκαμψη detour 3b
παραλία beach 16c
Παρασκευή Friday 8c
πάστα tart 13c
πάστα αμυγδάλου almond tart 13c
παστίτσιο macaroni dish 12b
(οι) πατάτες potatoes 13a
πατάτες τηγανητές potato chips 139
ΠΕΖΟΔΡΟΜΟΣ pedestrian zone 4c
Πέμπτη Thursday 8c
πενήντα fifty 7a
πεντακόσια five hundred 7a
πέντε five 7a
(το) πεπόνι honeydew melon 13b
περιοδεία tour (formal) 16a
πετσέτα towel 19d
πηγαίνω I go 16d
πηγαίνετε ευθεία go straight ahead 4d
(το) πηρούνι fork 10b
πιάτο plate 10b
πινακοθήκη art gallery 15b

(το) πιπέρι pepper 11c
πιπεριές (bell) peppers 13a
πισίνα swimming pool 16c
(η) πιστωτική κάρτα credit card 9b
(η) πλαζ beach 16c
πλατεία square 4c
(οι) ΠΛΗΡΟΦΟΡΙΕΣ information 5e
πληρώνω I pay 11d
(η) πόλη city, town 4b
πολύ very 1b, a lot 7b
πολυθρόνα deck-chair 16c
πονόδοντος toothache 20c
πορτοκαλάδα orangeade 14a
(το) πορτοκάλι orange 13b
(το) πορτ-μπαγκάς boot (of a car) 2a
(το) πρατήριο βενζίνης petrol station 3b
πόσο; How much ...? 7b
πότε ...; when ...? 8a, 15d
πόσο καιρό παίρνει how long does it take? 8c
πόσα; how many ...? 7b
(τα) ποτά drinks/beverages 14a
(το) ποτάμι river 16b
(το) ποτήρι glass 10b
Που είναι ...; Where is ...? 4d, 15a
(το) πουλόβερ pullover/sweater 19a
πουκάμισο shirt 19a
πράσινο green 19c
πρεσβεία embassy 2c
(το) πρόγευμα breakfast 6c
(το) πρόγραμμα programme 15c
ΠΡΟΕΛΕΥΣΗ origin 5e
προξενείο consulate 2c
ΠΡΟΟΡΙΣΜΟΣ destination 5e
ΠΡΟΣΟΧΗ caution! 3b
(το) προσπέκτους brochure 15a
(το) πρωί morning 8b
πρωινό breakfast 10a
πτήση flight 5b
πυρετός fever 20d
πως ...; how ...? 12b, 17a

(τα) ραδίκια greens (wild) 13a
(τα) ρεβύθια chick-peas 13a
ρετσίνα retsina 14b

Greek – English Vocabulary

(τα) ροδάκινα peaches 13b
(το) ρολόι clock, watch 8a
(το) ρύζι rice 13a
ρυζόγαλο rice pudding 13c

Σάββατο Saturday 8c
σάλτσα sauce 12b
(το) σαμπουάν shampoo 19d
(το) σάντουιτς sandwich 10d
(το) σαπούνι soap 19d
σαράντα forty 7a
(οι) σερβιέτες υγείας sanitary
   towels 19d
σήμερα today 8b, 17a
σιδηρόδρομος railway 5a
(το) σινεμά cinema 15b
σκέτο(ς) καφέ(ς) black coffee 10c
σκορδαλιά garlic sauce 13a
σκόρδο garlic 11c, 13a
(η) Σκωτία Scotland 2c
(ο) Σκωτσέζος Scottish (man) 2c
(η) Σκωτσέζα Scottish (woman) 2c
(τα) σλάϊτς slides 16d
σοκολάτα chocolate 14a
(το) σουβλάκι souvlaki 10d
σούπα soup 12a
σούπα ημέρας soup of the day 12a
(το) σορτ shorts 19a
(το) σπανάκι spinach 13a
(τα) σπίρτα matches 14c
(το) στάδιο stadium 15b
σταθμός (train) station 5a
ΣΤΑΘΜΟΣ ΤΑΞΙ taxi stand 5d
(η) ΣΤΑΣΗ (bus) stop 5d
(τα) σταφύλια grapes 13b
στιγμή moment 8a
στη γωνία at the corner 4d
στην υγειά σας cheers! 14b
στρίψετε δεξιά Turn right 4d
στρίψετε αριστερά Turn left 4d
(το) στρώμα φουσκωτό air mattress
   16c
στυλό ballpoint pen 18b
σύγκρουση collision 20a
(τα) σύκα figs 13b

(το) συνάλλαγμα currency exchange
   9b
συννεφιά cloudy 17c
ΣΥΡΑΤΕ pull! 9c

ΤΑΒΕΡΝΑ tavern (restaurant) 11a
ταμείο cashier, cash desk 9d
(το) ταξί taxi 5d
(το) ταξίδι trip 2a, 15a
ταραγμένη rough (sea) 17c
(ο) ταραμά(ς) fish roe 12d
ταραμοσαλάτα taramasalata (fish
   roe salad) 10d
(το) τασάκι ashtray 14c
ταχεία express train 5a
ΤΑΧΥΔΡΟΜΕΙΟ post office 18a
ταχύτητα speed 3a
ΤΕΛΩΝΕΙΑΚΟΣ ΕΛΕΓΧΟΣ cus-
   toms inspection 2a
ΤΕΛΩΝΕΙΟ customs 2a
(το) τέννις tennis 16c
τέσσερα four 7a
Τετάρτη Wednesday 8c
τετρακόσια four hundred 7a
(το) τζατζίκι yoghurt with garlic and
   cucumber 13a
(το) τζην jeans 19a
(το) τηλεγράφημα telegram 18c, 19a
(ο) τηλεφωνικός κατάλογος telephone directory 18c
τηλέφωνο telephone, telephone
   number 18c
τίποτα anything, nothing 2a
Τι κάνεις How are you? (informal)
   1b
Τι κάνετε; How are you? (formal)
   1b
τιμή price 6c, 9d
(το) τιρμπουσόν corkscrew 14b
(το) ΤΜΗΜΑ ΑΠΟΛΕΣΘΕΝΤΩΝ
   lost property office 20b
τόνος tuna 12d
(το) τοστ toast 10d
(η) τουαλέττα toilet 6d
τραυματίστηκα I am injured 20c
τσιγάρο cigarette 14c

Greek – English Vocabulary

(ο) τουρίστας tourist (man) 15a
(η) τουρίστρια tourist (woman) 15a
(ο) τουριστικός οδηγός tourist guide 15a
Τουριστική Αστυνομία Tourist Police 15a
τράβελερς τσέκ traveller's cheque 9b
τραίνο train 5a
τράπεζα bank 9b
(το) τραπέζι table 11a
τρία three 7a
τριακόσια three hundred 7a
τριάντα thirty 7a
Τρίτη Tuesday 8c
τροχόσπιτο trailer 3a
(το) τσάι tea 10c, 14a
τσάι με γάλα tea with milk 10c
τσάι με λεμόνι tea with lemon 10c
τσάντα handbag 2a
τσατσάρα comb 19e
τσιπούρα snapper (fish) 12d
τσιρότο sticking plaster 20e
(το) τυρί cheese 10d
τυρόπιτα cheese pastry 10d

υπηκοότητα nationality 2c
(το) υποβρύχιο ψάρεμα under-water fishing 16d
υπογραφή signature 2b

(τα) φαγητά food 10a
φάκελος envelope 18b
(οι) φακές lentils 13a
(το) φανάρι traffic light 4c
φαρμακείο chemist, pharmacy 20e
φάρμακο medicine 20c
(τα) φασόλια beans 13a
(τα) φασολάκια φρέσκα runner beans 13a
(το) φεριμπότ ferryboat 5c
(το) φεστιβάλ κρασιού wine festival 15b
φέτα féta cheese 10d
φιλέτο fillet steak 12b
(το) φιλμ film 16c

φλάουτο flute 15c
(το) φλας (photo) flash 16d
(το) φλιτζάνι cup 10b
φούστα skirt 19a
(το) φόρεμα dress 19a
(οι) φράουλες strawberries 13b
(το) φραπέ coffee with ice cream 14
(τα) φρούτα fruit 13b
φυσάει αέρας It is windy 17d
φτηνό cheap 9d
(τα) φυστίκια pistachio nuts 13b
φωτογραφία photograph 16d
φωτογραφική μηχανή camera 16d

χαίρετε hello/goodbye (formal) 1b
(το) χαλάζι hail 17d
(το) χάπι pill 20e
(τα) χαρτομάντηλα tissues 19d
(ο) χάρτης map 4a
χάρτης της Ελλάδας map of Greece 4a
χθες yesterday 8b
χίλια thousand 7a
χιλιόμετρο kilometer 7b
χιόνι snow 17d
(τα) χόρτα greens 13a
χρόνος time, year 8c
(το) χταπόδι octopus 12d
(το) χρώμα colour 19c
(ο) χυμός φρούτου fruit juice 10c, 14a
χτένα comb 19c
χωρίς without 14a

(το) ψάρι fish 12d
ψάρι πλακί stewed fish 12d
ψάρι στο φούρνο baked fish 12d
ψάρι τηγανητό fried fish 12d
ψάρι στη σχάρα grilled fish 12d
ψάρι στα κάρβουνα fish baked o charcoal 12d
ψαρόσουπα fish soup 12a
ΨΑΡΟΤΑΒΕΡΝΑ taverna special ising in seafood 11a
(τα) ψιλά small change 9a

Greek – English Vocabulary

ΨΗΣΤΑΡΙΑ taverna specializing in charcoal-grilled food 11a

(το) ψωμάκι roll 10c

(το) ψωμί bread 10c

ΩΘΗΣΑΤΕ push 9c

ώρα hour 8a

(οι) ώρες λειτουργίας opening hours 15d

English – Greek Vocabulary

address διεύθυνση 2b
admission ticket εισιτήριο 15d
afternoon απόγευμα 8b
airmail αεροπορικώς 18b
air mattress στρώμα φουσκωτό 16c
airport αεροδρόμιο 5b
airport αερολιμένας (formal) 5b
a little λίγο 7b
almonds αμύγδαλα 13b
a lot πολύ 7b
America (U.S.A.) Αμερική 2c
American (man) Αμερικάνος 2c
American (woman) Αμερικανίδα 2c
American (adjective) αμερικάνικος 2c
ambulance ασθενοφόρο 20f
amphitheatre αμφιθέατρο 15b
amphora αμφορέας 15b
and you (formal) κι εσείς 1b
and you (informal) κι εσύ 1b
anything τίποτα 2a
antiquities αρχαία 15b
appetisers ορεκτικά 12a
apple μήλο 13b
apple pie μηλόπιτα 13c
arrival (times) αφίξεις 5e
art gallery πινακοθήκη 15b
artichoke αγκινάρα 13a
ashtray τασάκι 14c
attention! προσοχή! 20g
aubergine μελιτζάνα 13a
Australia Αυστραλία 2c
Australian (man) Αυστραλός 2c
Australian (woman) Αυστραλέζα 2c
avenue λεωφόρος 4c

bad weather άσχημος καιρός 17c
ballpoint pen στυλό 18b
bandage επίδεσμος 20e
bank τράπεζα 9b
barber's ΚΟΥΡΕΙΟ 19e
bath μπάνιο 6b
bathing suit/trunks μαγιό 19a
battery μπαταρία 16d
beach παραλία 16c
beach umbrella ομπρέλλα ηλίου 16c
beans φασόλια 13a

bed κρεβάτι 6b
beer μπύρα 14b
belt ζώνη 19a
beverages ποτά 14a
bikini μπικίνι 19a
bill λογαριασμό(ς) 6c, 11d
black μαύρο 19c
blouse μπλούζα 19a
blue μπλε 19c
boot (of a car) πορτ-μπαγκάζ 2a
boat καράβι 5c
bottle μπουκάλι 10b
bouzouki μπουζούκι 15c
bread ψωμί 10c
breakdown βλάβη 20a
breakfast πρωινό 10a
brochure προσπέκτους 15a
brown καφέ 19c
bus λεωφορείο 5d
butcher's shop ΚΡΕΟΠΩΛΕΙΟ 10c
butter βούτυρο 10c

cabbage λάχανο 13a
café καφενείο 11c
cake κέϊκ 13c
calm sea ήρεμη 17c
camera φωτογραφική μηχανή 16d
campsite κάμπινγκ 6a
can I ... ? μπορώ να ... ? 18c
Canada Καναδάς 2c
Canadian (man) Καναδός 2c
Canadian (woman) Καναδέζα 2c
canoe κανώ 16c
cappuccino καπουτσίνο 14a
car αυτοκίνητο 3a
car registration papers άδεια οδηγήσεως 2b
car rental ενοικειάσεις αυτοκινήτων 3a
caravan τροχόσπιτο 3a
carrots καρότα 13a
cashier ταμείο 9d
chair καρέκλα 11a
catacombs κατακόμβες 15b
cauliflower κουνουπίδι 13a
caution! ΠΡΟΣΟΧΗ 3b
changeable weather αστάθεια 17c

English – Greek Vocabulary

changing rooms δοκιμαστήρια 19a
cheap φτηνό 9d
cheers! στην υγειά σας! 14b
cheese τυρί 10d
cheese pastry τυρόπιτα 10d
chemist φαρμακείο 20e
cheque τσέκ 9b
cherries κεράσια 13b
chicken κότα 12a
(young) chicken κοτόπουλο 12a
chicken soup κοτόσουπα 12a
chick-peas ρεβύθια 13a
chocolate σοκολάτα 13c
church εκκλησία 15b
cigarette τσιγάρο 14c
cinema κινηματογράφος or σινεμά 15b
city πόλη 4b
city map χάρτης της πόλης 4a
clean καθαρός 16c
clear καθαρός 17b
classical Greek tragedy αρχαία ελληνική τραγωδία 15b
clock ρολόι 8a
closed κλειστό 9c
cloudy συννεφιά 17c
cocoa σοκολάτα 14a
cod μπακαλιάρος 12d
coffee καφέ(ς) 10c, 14a
coffee with ice cream φραπέ 14a
coin κέρμα 9a
colour χρώμα 19c
cold (weather) κρύο 17d
collision σύγκρουση 20a
colour film έγχρωμο φίλμ 16d
column κολώνα 15b
comb τσατσαρα, κτένα, 19e
complete, fixed price meal μενού 11b
cognac κονιάκ 14b
consulate προξενείο 2c
coast ακτή 16b
cool (weather) δροσιά 17d
corkscrew τιρμπουσόν 14b
corner γωνία 4d
courgettes κολοκυθάκια 13a
crayfish καραβίδες 12d
credit card πιστωτική κάρτα 9b
cucumber αγγούρι 13a

cup φλυτζάνι 10b
currency exchange συνάλλαγμα 9b
customs τελωνείο 2a
customs inspection τελωνειακό έλεγχος 2a
cutlets παϊδάκια 12b

danger κίνδυνος 20a
date ημερομηνία 2b
day μέρα 6b
for how many days για πόσες μέρες 6b
deep βαθειά 16d
dentist οδοντογιατρός 20f
departure (times) αναχωρήσεις 5c
desserts γλυκά 13c
destination προορισμός 5e
detour παράκαμψη 3b
dinner δείπνο 10a
doctor γιατρός 20f
dollar δολλάριο 9b
dolmades ντολμάδες 10d
dolphin δελφίνι 16b
double room διπλό δωμάτιο 6b
drachma δραχμή 9a
drama δράμα 15c
dress φόρεμα 19a
drinks ποτά 14a
driver οδηγός 3a
driver's licence άδεια οδηγήσεως 2b
dry wine κρασί ξηρό 14b

egg αυγό 12a
eight οχτώ 7a
eight hundred οχτακόσια 7a
eighteen δέκα-οχτώ 7a
eighty ογδόντα 7a
electric razor ηλεκτρική ξυριστική μηχανή 19d
eleven έν-δεκα 7a
embassy πρεσβεία 2c
Emergency Exit ΕΞΟΔΟΣ ΚΙΝΔΥΝΟΥ 20g
emergency telephone τηλέφωνο βοηθείας ατυχημάτων 20a

English – Greek Vocabulary

England Αγγλία 2c
English (man) Άγγλος 2c
English (woman) Αγγλίδα 2c
English (adjective) αγγλικός 2c
English (language) Αγγλικά 2c
entrance είσοδος 5d
envelope φάκελος 18b
espresso εσπρέσσο 14a
evening βράδυ 8b
excursion εκδρομή 16a
exhibition έκθεση 15b
excuse me με συγχωρείτε 1d
exit έξοδος 5d
expensive ακριβό 9d
express train ταχεία 5a

fair (weather) αίθριος 17b
ferryboat φεριμπότ 5c
feta cheese φέτα τυρί 10d
fever πυρετός 20d
fifteen δέκα-πέντε 7a
fifty πενήντα 7a
figs σύκα 13b
fillet (steak) φιλέτο 12b
film φιλμ 16c
fish ψάρι 12d
fish stewed ψάρι πλακί 12d
fish baked ψάρι στο φούρνο 12d
fish fried ψάρι τηγανητό 12d
fish grilled ψάρι στη σχάρα 12d
fish baked on charcoal ψάρι στα
κάρβουνα 12d
fish roe ταραμάς 12d
fish soup ψαρόσουπα 12a
five πέντε 7a
five hundred πεντακόσια 7a
flight πτήση 5b
floor όροφος 6b
flute φλάουτο 15c
fog ομίχλη 17d
folk dancing λαϊκός χορός 15b
food φαγητό 10a
foreigner αλλοδαπός 2c
fork πηρούνι 10b
forty σαράντα 7a
four τέσσερα 7a
four hundred τετρακόσια 7a

fourteen δέκα-τέσσερα 7a
Friday Παρασκευή 8c
fruit φρούτο 13b
fruit juice χυμός φρούτου 10b, 14a

garage γκαράζ 20a
garlic σκόρδο 13a
garlic sauce σκορδαλιά 13a
(I) give δίνω 11c
glass ποτήρι 10b
(I) go πηγαίνω 16d
goodbye (formal) χαίρετε 1b
goodbye (informal) γειά σου 1b
good evening καλησπέρα 1b
good morning καλημέρα 1b
good night καληνύχτα 1b
good weather καλός καιρός 17b
grapes σταφύλια 13b
Greece Ελλάδα 2a
Greek (man) Έλληνας 2c
Greek (woman) Ελληνίδα 2c
Greek (adjective) ελληνικός 2c
Greek (language) Ελληνικά 2b
green πράσινο 19c
grey γκρι 19c
ground floor ισόγειο 6b
(tourist) guide ξεναγός 15d
gulf κόλπος 16b

hairdresser κομμωτήριο 19e
handbag τσάντα 2a
handkerchief μαντήλι 19d
hail χαλάζι 17d
harbour λιμάνι 5c
hat καπέλο 19a
hello (formal) χαίρετε 1b
hello (informal) γειά σου 1b
help βοήθεια 20g
here εδώ 4d
hospital νοσοκομείο 20f
hot (weather) ζέστη 17b
hotel ξενοδοχείο 6a
hour ώρα 8a
How are you? (formal) Τι κάνετε; 1b
How are you? (informal) Τι κάνεις;
1b

English – Greek Vocabulary

How many...? πόσα 7b
How much...? πόσο 6c, 9d, 18b
How long...? πόσο καιρό 8c
husband άντρας 1f

I εγώ 1f
ice cream παγωτό 13c
icon εικόνα 15b
ill άρρωστος 20d
information πληροφορίες 5e
(I am) injured τραυματίστηκα 20c
insurance ασφάλεια 20a
interpreter διερμηνέα(ς) 20c
island νησί 16b
isthmus ισθμός 16b
It's alright εντάξει 11d

jacket ζακέτα 19a
jeans τζην 19a

key κλειδί 6b
kid (young goat) κατσικάκι 12b
kilo κιλό 7d
kilometre χιλιόμετρο 7b
knife μαχαίρι 10d

lamp αρνάκι 12b
last week Την περασμένη εβδομάδα 8c
lawyer δικηγόρος 20c
left αριστερά 4d
left luggage office γραφείο αποσκευών 5a
lemon λεμόνι 13b
lemonade λεμονάδα 14a
lentils φακές 13a
letter γράμμα 18b
lettuce μαρούλι 13a
lifeguard ακτοφύλακας 16c
lift ασανσέρ 6b
lighter αναπτήρας 14c
lightning αστραπή 16d

(I) like (it) μ' αρέσει 19b
(I) like (them) μ' αρέσουν 19b
liqueur λικέρ 14b
litre λίτρο 7b
(I) live μένω 4b
lobster αστακός 12d
look out! προσοχή! 20g
lost property office τμήμα απολεσθέντων 20b
luggage αποσκευές 2a
lunch γεύμα 10a

mailbox γραμματοκιβώτιο 18b
map χάρτης 4a
map of Greece χάρτης της Ελλάδας 4a
market αγορά 9c
marmalade μαρμελάδα 10c
matches σπίρτα 14c
meat κρέας 12b
meatballs κεφτέδες 12b
medicine φάρμακο 20l
Mediterranean Sea Μεσόγειος Θάλασσα 16b
medium μέτριο 12b
melon πεπόνι 13b
MEN (toilet) ΑΝΔΡΩΝ 6d
menu κατάλογος 11b
metre μέτρο 7b
milk γάλα 14a
mineral water μεταλλικό νερό 14a
minute λεπτό 8a
Miss δεσποινίς 1d
moment στιγμή 8a
monastery μοναστήρι 15b
Monday Δευτέρα 8c
money λεφτά 9a
month μήνας 8c
morning πρωί 8b
motor boat βάρκα με μηχανή 16c
motorway εθνική οδός 3b
mountain βουνό 16b
moussaka μουσακά(ς) 12b
Mr. κύριος 1d
Mrs. κυρία 1d
museum μουσείο 15b
mutton αρνάκι 12b

English – Greek Vocabulary

name όνομα 2b
nationality υπηκοότητα 2c
new νέα 4b
newspaper εφημερίδα 2c
next week την άλλη εβδομάδα 8c
night νύχτα 8b
(for one night για μία νύχτα) 6b
nine εννιά 7a
nine hundred εννιακόσια 7a
nineteen δεκα-εννιά 7a
ninety ενενήντα 7a
no όχι 1a
no (parking) απαγορεύεται η
  στάθμευση 3d
No through road ΑΔΙΕΞΟΔΟΣ 3c
noon μεσημέρι 8b
No smoking μή καπνίζετε 14c
nothing τίποτα 2a
number αριθμός 7b

octopus χταπόδι 12d
of course βέβαια 11a
oil λάδι 3c 11c
ointment αλοιφή 20e
old αρχαία 4b
olives ελιές 13a
omelette ομελέττα 12c
one ένα 7a
one-way traffic μονόδρομος 3b
onions κρεμμύδια 13a
open ανοικτό 9c
opening hours ώρες λειτουργίας 15d
orange πορτοκάλι 13b
orangeade πορτοκαλάδα 14a
origin προέλευση 5e
ouzo ούζο 14b
over there εκεί πέρα 6d

pack of cigarettes ένα πακέτο
  τσιγάρα 14c
pair ζευγάρι 19b
parcels ΔΕΜΑΤΑ 18b
passport διαβατήριο 2b
passport control Έλεγχος
  διαβατηρίου 2b

pastry shop Ζαχαροπλαστείο 11a
(I) pay πληρώνω 11d
peaches ροδάκινα 13b
pears αχλάδια 13b
peas μπιζέλια 13a
people άτομα 6b
pepper πιπέρι 11c
(bell) peppers πιπεριές 13a
petrol βενζίνη 3c
petrol station πρατήριο βενζίνης 3b
pharmacy φαρμακείο 20e
photograph φωτογραφία 16d
pill χάπι 20e
pistachio nuts φυστίκια 13b
plate πιάτο 10b
please παρακαλώ 1c
police αστυνομία 20c
porter! Αχθοφόρε 5a
postcard κάρτα 18b
post office ταχυδρομείο 18a
potatoes πατάτες 13a
pound λίρα 9b
price τιμή 6c, 9d
price of the room τιμή δωματίου 6c
programme πρόγραμμα 15c
pull σύρατε 9c
push ωθήσατε 9c

quickly γρήγορα 20c

rail car αυτοκινητάμαξα 5a
railroad σιδηρόδρομος 5a
rain βροχή 17c
It is raining βρέχει 17c
receipt απόδειξη 11d
red κόκκινο 19c
red mullet μπαρμπούνι 12d
red wine κόκκινο κρασί 14b
refreshments αναψυκτικά 14a
restaurant εστιατόριο 11a
retsina ρετσίνα 14b
rice ρύζι 13a
rice pudding ρυζόγαλο 13c
right δεξιά 4d
river ποτάμι 16b
road δρόμος 3b

English – Greek Vocabulary

robbery κλοπή 20b
roll ψωμάκι 10c
room δωμάτιο 6b
rough sea κυματώδης θάλασσα 17c
rowing boat βάρκα 16c
runner beans φασολάκια φρέσκα 13a

sailing boat βάρκα με πανί 16c
saint άγιος 15b
salt αλάτι 11c
sand άμμος 16c
sandwich σάντουϊτς 10d
sanitary towels σερβιέτες υγείας 19d
Saturday Σάββατο 8c
sauce σάλτσα 12b
Scotland Σκωτία 2c
Scottish (man) Σκωτσέζος 2c
Scottish (woman) Σκωτσέζα 2c
sea θάλασσα 16b
seat θέση 5e
seven εφτά 7a
seven hundred εφτακόσια 7a
seventeen δεκα-εφτά 7a
seventy εβδομήντα 7a
shampoo σαμπουάν 19d
shark καρχαρίας 16b
shirt πουκάμισο 19a
shoes παπούτσια 19b
shop κατάστημα 9c
shorts σόρτ 19a
shower ντους 6b
shrimps γαρίδες 12d
sick άρρωστος 20d
signature υπογραφή 2b
single room μονό δωμάτιο 6b
six έξι 7a
six hundred εξακόσια 7a
sixteen δεκα-έξι 7a
sixty εξήντα 7a
size μέγεθος 19a
skirt φούστα 19a
sleeping car κλινάμαξα 5d
slides σλάϊτς 16d
small change ψιλά 9a
snack μεζέδες 10d

soap σαπούνι 19d
socks κάλτσες 19b
soup σούπα 12a
soup of the day σούπα ημέρας 12a
souvlaki σουβλάκι 10d
(I) speak μιλώ 2c
special offer ειδική προσφορά 9c
speed ταχύτητα 3a
spinach σπανάκι 13a
spoon κουτάλι 10b
square πλατεία 4c
squid καλαμαράκια 12d
stadium στάδιο 15b
stamps γραμματόσημα 18b
starters ΜΕΖΕΔΕΣ 12a
(train) station σταθμός 5a
statue άγαλμα 15b
steak φιλέτο 12b
steamer βαπόρι 5c
(bus) stop στάση 5d
stockings κάλτσες 19b
storm θύελλα 17c
straight ahead ευθεία 4d
strawberries φράουλες 13b
street οδός 4c
street map οδικός χάρτης 4a
sugar ζάχαρη 11c
suitcase βαλίτσα 2a
sun ήλιος 17b
Sunday Κυριακή 8c
sunglasses γυαλιά ηλίου 19d
sunshine λιακάδα 17b
sunstroke ηλίαση 20d
suntan cream κρέμα ηλίου 19d
suntan oil λάδι ηλίου 19d
sweater πουλόβερ 19a
sweets γλυκά 13c
sweet wine γλυκό κρασί 14b
swimming κολύμπι 16d
swimming pool πισίνα 16c

table τραπέζι 11a
tavern (restaurant) ταβέρνα 11a
taxi ταξί 5d
taxi stand σταθμός ταξί 5d
tea τσάι 10c, 14a
telegram τηλεγράφημα 18c

English – Greek Vocabulary

telephone τηλέφωνο 18c
telephone directory τηλεφωνικός
  κατάλογος 18c
temperature θερμοκρασία 17a
temple ναός 15b
ten δέκα 7a
tennis τέννις 16c
thank you ευχαριστώ 1c
the ο, η, τό 1e
theatre θέατρο 15b
there εκεί 4d
there is υπάρχει 6a
thirteen δεκα-τρία 7a
thirty τριάντα 7a
this αυτός 1e
three τρία 7a
three hundred τριακόσια 7a
thunderstorm καταιγίδα 17c
Thursday Πέμπτη 8c
tickets εισιτήρια 5e
tights καλσόν 19b
time χρόνος 8c
timetable ΔΡΟΜΟΛΟΓΙΑ 5e
tissues χαρτομάντηλα 19d
toast τόστ 10d
today σήμερα 8b
toilet τουαλέττα 6d
toll διόδια 3b
tomato ντομάτα 13a
tomato soup ντοματόσουπα 12a
tomorrow αύριο 8b
toothache πονόδοντος 20c
toothbrush οδοντόβουρτσα 19d
toothpaste οδοντόκρεμα 19d
tour (formal) περιοδεία 16a
tour (informal) γύρος 16a
tourist (man) τουρίστας 15a
tourist (woman) τουρίστρια 15a
tourist office Γραφείο Τουρισμού
  15a
Tourist Police Τουριστική
  Αστυνομία 15a
tourist guide τουριστικός οδηγός
  15a
towel πετσέτα 19d
town centre κέντρο 4b
track γραμμή 5a
traffic οδική κυκλοφορία 3a

traffic light φανάρι 4c
train τραίνο 5a
traveller's cheque τράβελερς τσέκ 9b
trip ταξίδι 2a, 15a
trousers πανταλόνι 19a
Tuesday Τρίτη 8c
tuna τόνος 12b
turn left στρίψετε αριστερά 4d
turn right στρίψετε δεξιά 4d
twelve δώδεκα 7a
two δύο 7a

vanilla βανίλια 13c
vase βάζο 9c
veal μοσχαράκι 12a
vegetables λαχανικά 13a
very πολύ 1b

waiter γκαρσόν 11d
waiting room αίθουσα αναμονής 5a
Wales Ουαλλία 2c
Welsh (man) Ουαλλός 2c
Welsh (woman) Ουαλλέζα 2c
(I) want θέλω 3a
warm (weather) ζέστη 17b
water νερό 10b, 14a
water melon καρπούζι 13b
water-skiing θαλάσσιο σκί 16c
weather καιρός 17a
Wednesday Τετάρτη 8c
week εβδομάδα 8c
well καλά 1b
what τι 5c
what time …? τι ώρα … 5c, 8b
where is …? που είναι …? 4d
white άσπρο 19c
white wine άσπρο κρασί 14b
wife γυναίκα 1f
wind (colloquial) αέρας 17c
wind (formal) άνεμος 17c
(It is) windy φυσάει αέρας 17c
wine κρασί 14b
wine festival φεστιβάλ 15b
with με 10c
with milk με γάλα 10c
with lemon με λεμόνι 10c
without χωρίς 14a

English – Greek Vocabulary

WOMEN (toilet) τουαλέττα
  γυναικών 6d
word λέξη 18d

year χρόνος 8c
yellow κίτρινο 19c
yes ναι 1a

yesterday χθές 8b
yoghurt γιαούρτι 10d
yoghurt with garlic and cucumber
  τζατζίκι 13a
you (formal) εσείδ 1f

zero μηδέν 7a

Notes

Notes

Notes

Also available in this series

Quick & Easy French
Quick & Easy German
Quick & Easy Italian
Quick & Easy Spanish

TEACH YOURSELF BOOKS